JOHN OWENS

Banish
WORRY
AND
ANXIETY
Forever

7 SIMPLE STEPS to better focus,
health, and relationships in just
30 MINUTES A DAY

Contents

Free Gift!

As a thank-you for getting this book, I'd like to give you a free gift: a unique Zen12 guided meditation audio download.

To get the very best from the LENSE+GP method, with the least amount of effort, it is essential that you download and use your FREE Zen12 meditation with brainwave entrainment MP3 audio.

This will help to do most, if not all, of the hard work for you.

Using the highly specialized Zen12 audio means that you can avoid having to spend a whole lifetime learning the meditation techniques necessary to consistently achieve the deeply relaxed state of mind required to apply, successfully, the special thought control technique described in this book.

Of course, if you should wish to do so, you could choose to use a traditional style of meditation instead of the Zen12 audio. To facilitate this, you will find a meditation has been provided for you in the Appendix.

The Appendix has been provided assuming you are new to meditation. It incorporates progressive muscle relaxation techniques developed by Dr. Edmund Jacobson in the 1930s[56,57] to reduce his patients' anxiety levels, help them overcome fatigue, and enable them to think more rationally.

The FREE Zen12 download audio has been specially arranged with the UK producer and provider of this highly respected, specialized software, for the readers of this book, via our website.

To access your own FREE downloadable copy of the brainwave-enhanced Zen12 guided meditation track, simply download it by going direct to the website at:

https://www.zen12.com/gift/a/thebestyou

or alternatively visit our website:

https://www.thebestyouprogramme.com/book/free-mp3

where you can register for free updates, other helpful resources, and FREE information – so register… download… enjoy!

Acknowledgements

There are many people I need to acknowledge and express my genuine appreciation to, for their guidance and support in making this book a reality.

They include the inspirational Christopher John Payne for his guidance and access to his tried and trusted Effort-Free Online Success system (EFOS), to Ken Leeder who designed and provided the cover and Naomi Munts who took my draft and formatted it into something that could be published using the EFOS, and to the many professionals along the way for sharing their vast knowledge and expertise with me over the years.

To Sarah Staar, at Sarah Staar Business School, and Rob Cornish of *Gain Higher Ground* and of "Nano Product" creation fame, for collectively introducing me to Chris Payne.

To my father who sadly just passed away at 99 years of age and instilled within me the values of honesty and integrity.

To my much-loved and dearly missed mother who was an exceptional person and loved me unconditionally since my birth, and to whom I dedicate this book in her memory, for despite all of her many virtues, she might just have been one of the world's greatest worriers, which in a strange indirect way is what may have ultimately (and in all probability) cost her her life.

And to my wife Sheila, who has always supported me, despite the many challenges of doing so, and who provided me with the greatest gift possible when she brought into this world life in the form of our two much-loved sons.

Author's Note

Although JAM Internet Marketing Ltd and Publishing is based in the UK, this edition of the book has been edited to align with English used in the United States of America and some other locations, where some words are spelled differently than the English used in the UK.

For example: neighbor instead of neighbour, behavior instead of behaviour, favorite instead of favourite, color instead of colour, analyze instead of analyse, diarrhea instead of diarrhoea, humor instead of humour, organization instead of organisation.

Please don't be irritated or annoyed or distracted by this. If you are in the UK and require a British English spelling edition of the book, please drop us an email to our website and we will be pleased to provide you with an English PDF version of the book FREE of charge (just include proof of purchase with your email).

Thank you for your understanding and we truly hope you will enjoy and get the very best from the book.

Foreword and Introduction

Foreword and Introduction

Firstly, congratulations to you for taking your first step along the path that leads you to being free from worry and anxiety, and from the very serious negative consequences they have on your physical and mental wellbeing.

I know from personal experience what it is like to summon the courage and commitment necessary to take that first step, when you are suffering the pain, anguish, and dread of the consequences of worry and anxiety.

For me it was a bit like trying to swim against a fierce and never-ending current, and while you know that you're not getting anywhere, you keep on swimming regardless, and then feel so exhausted, hopeless, and full of despair.

Indeed, swimming against any fierce current, even if you are an Olympian swimmer, is not only futile and pointless, it can have very serious and perhaps even fatal consequences for you, or a loved one.

Of course, to someone outside of your circumstances and situation, it might be blindingly obvious that it is pointless and futile swimming against a fierce current, and that what you need to do is to work with the current, let it help you and take you to a place of safety.

I appreciate this is not a perfect analogy, but it may help in gaining another perspective on what can otherwise become a complex subject area.

As you will discover in this book, the reality is that if you are suffering from the very real *negative physiological, emotional, cognitive, or behavioral consequences* that result from worry and anxiety, it can be very hard for you to logically evaluate your situation and take the necessary action to improve your state or circumstances.

When you are struggling with fear, dread, or physical or emotional pain and suffering, what you also don't need is to hear someone tell you that you just need to *snap out of it*, or to *get over it*, or *forget about it and move on.*

You will know only too well that this just doesn't help you one little bit as you simply don't have the energy, or the peace of mind, that is necessary for you to be able to focus and determine the actual cause of your worry and anxiety, let alone work out how to improve your circumstances or situation, or how to banish them forever.

Is it any wonder then if, like me, when you tried the classical *distraction techniques*, or the popular *avoidance behavior* or resisting approaches (or the mind-numbingly slow therapy sessions that soak up all your energy, time, and money), they just somehow failed to really help you?

Some experiences of traditional therapies and methods

Even the expensive therapy sessions I took failed to have any long-lasting benefit.

As you will discover shortly, almost immediately following what benefit you do get from such an approach, your dominant neural pathway and egoic mind will make sure you end up right back where you started.

Even worse, if this experience is repeated, it will have a reinforcing effect on your neural pathways, making it even harder for you to break free from your worry and anxiety (see the chapter on the principal causes of your worry and anxiety).

Now, to be very clear, please do not substitute this book for (or drop out of) any professional therapy that you might be lucky enough to secure and afford, and to be courageous enough to put yourself through.

I did all of these things and, for me, all it did was leave me exhausted, frustrated, annoyed, and angry, feeling suffocated and overwhelmed and even more worried and anxious than before.

I just knew there must be another, better way.

However, here at last is some very good news, and I am living proof (if proof was needed) that it doesn't have to be like that.

You can now escape, just as I did, and leave all of this behind you.

I can tell you from my own personal experience, it really doesn't have to be like this – you can now do something about it, to live a *normal, confident, independent, successful, and healthier life*. Yes, you really can *banish your worry and anxiety forever*.

A proven new science – and technology – based method

There is now a new science – and technology – based proven way (which has predictable and repeatable results) to control your thoughts and emotions, and therefore your actions and results, even if you have a very busy corporate or hectic lifestyle or career and you don't have the time, or energy, for expensive therapy sessions.

And it doesn't matter whether you, like me, have lived most of your life suffering from the *significant negative consequences* to *your physical and mental wellbeing from worry and anxiety*, or whether it has suddenly and unexpectedly grabbed hold of you, and you are wondering what is happening to you, or *"why me?"*, or *"what does all this mean?"* and *"what does my future now hold for me?"*

There is now a new, proven, science-based technology that has been specifically and purposely developed from some of the world's most advanced institutes to help interrupt the cycle of worry and anxiety and to calm the activity in your mind.

If this carefully selected and adapted technology is then used in a very specific way and combined with a particular proven mind-control technique, exactly as detailed in this book, it becomes a very simple-to-use, fast-track way to banish your worry and anxiety.

After two years of extensive research and much experimentation with various versions and combinations of technology, techniques, and methods, I eventually arrived at what I call my LENSE+GP method.

For me, this really is about as *effort free* as it gets, since it has at its very core some scientifically developed and proven technology that does most, if not all, of the work for you.

5

This allows you to skip the time-consuming learning and practice sessions you would otherwise have to endure to get similar results from a traditional or classical approach.

To ensure that you have access to this very specific and highly specialized brainwave-enhanced technology, we have arranged for you (readers of this book only) to access *a FREE downloadable audio*, from the UK producer and provider of this highly respected, specialized software, via the website at:

https://www.zen12.com/gift/a/thebestyou

You are not alone

Of course, your situation and life circumstances will depend upon a number of different and very unique (to you) factors; therefore you may be thinking that you are alone, that no one else will be suffering the way you are.

Sadly, that is not the case.

Studies, such as those published in the *Journal of Clinical Psychiatry* back in April 2000,[55] estimate that in America alone, approximately 27 million people have an anxiety disorder at some time in their life, and a more recent report by the Anxiety and Depression Association of America suggests that this figure has risen to some 40 million adults in the USA.

According to the World Health Organization in 2017, the total estimated number of people living with anxiety disorders in the world is 264 million, an increase of 14.9% since 2005.

So you are not alone, and it is certainly not in any way your fault.

For many years I thought it "normal" to have those sweaty palms, heart palpitations, nausea, crippling stomach pains, and diarrhea, and I felt the dread of having to interact with other people, or of what might become of me or a loved one.

I used to get so annoyed when someone would say, *You should stop worrying, it is not good for you*, or that *nothing helpful or good ever came from worrying*, or, *All that worry will make you ill.*

This never helped me at all; in fact, it just made me feel even more anxious and worried than ever, for reasons we will discover shortly.

Even though, of course, you know that they are right – after all, it makes perfect *logical* sense, doesn't it?

Just like it makes logical sense not to swim against a fierce current.

However, when you are so consumed with overwhelm by your thoughts and emotions, and you are struggling to survive, you simply don't have enough capacity, or the capability, to do what is needed to improve your situation or circumstances, or to escape from the negative consequences.

So, you will most probably just acknowledge that you *know this already* and continue living with all your worry and anxiety, regardless of the consequences.

Your worry and anxiety have very real consequences

And there are very real and long-term negative consequences – check out the chapter "The Significant Consequences of Your Worry and Anxiety" to see where you might be on the spectrum or scale of physical, emotional, cognitive, and behavioral consequences.

The ever-growing weight of scientific evidence and studies now clearly show there is an undeniable relationship between worry and anxiety and many significant physical and mental wellbeing issues.

I, like many others, thought that you could never escape from these negative consequences or their constant presence, and I therefore sought help and assistance from a very *highly respected and renowned European clinic* that specializes in behavioral and cognitive counselling and mental wellbeing.

Although it was very expensive (think thousands of dollars), it provided me with a coping strategy to *manage* my constant worry and anxiety. Although of some initial help, however, it proved to be of little lasting value in addressing the cause of my longstanding worry and anxiety.

This did, however, introduce me to, and provide me with, insights into to some of the traditional therapy strategies and techniques, one such therapy being the application of a structured MBCT program.

Potential benefits from some traditional therapies

Numerous research studies show that certain traditional therapies for resolving the negative consequences of your worry and anxiety, such as Cognitive Behavioral Therapy, when combined with a mindfulness meditation, known as Mindfulness-Based Cognitive Therapy (MBCT) and Mindfulness-Based Stress Reduction (MBSR), can provide you *with some very real and significant benefits.*[9,10,11,12]

Benefits that show that you are less likely to *die from a heart attack,*[5] and that you are *43% less likely* to suffer from a *repeat bout of depression*[10] or to experience the *pain of a destructive behavior, substance abuse, or self-harm,*[30,31] or to *suffer from digestive diseases, including irritable bowel syndrome* (IBS).[3,8]

You are able to relax, sharpen and focus your mind,[27] improve your memory and mood,[12, 22] master your emotions,[11,15] boost your energy levels and immune system,[12,28] lower your blood pressure,[15] and alleviate tension in your muscles.[3,15]

This program is now said to be the *preferred and recommended treatment in the UK*, by the government's official body that provides national guidance and advice to improve health and social care, known as the National Institute for Health and Care Excellence (NICE), to prevent depression in people who have had three or more bouts of depression in their past [20], and is said to be at least as good as drugs for the treatment of clinical-level depression. [15,41]

One study shows using MBCT typically reduced relapse rates to be (up to) a staggering 50%[11] and in another 43%.[10]

In fact, for those suffering from worry and anxiety, MBCT- and MBSR-based therapies can (eventually) positively impact almost all areas of your physical and psychological wellbeing, and some studies show that they are, in some cases, at least as good as prescribed drugs.[15,21]

The challenge

So, the challenge that this book sets out to solve was: *How can you obtain these benefits without the very considerable time and effort necessary to achieve them when using traditional methods, and in a way that provides predictable and consistent results, and takes less than 30 minutes a day to achieve?*

Firstly though, let me just say right up front that I am not a psychologist, nor a physician, or a professional medical practitioner or advisor; I am just a regular guy, an engineer by profession, who has lived for years with the condition and consequences of constant worry and anxiety.

Through desperation more than anything else, I became obsessed with finding a simple and easy-to-use method that would allow me to become free from all the constant worry and anxiety that kept me locked in its grip of pain and suffering, and from the physiological, emotional, cognitive, and behavioral consequences.

Consequences that you might experience at the physiological level are heart palpitations, clammy hands, sweating, irritability, muscle tension, concentration difficulties, indecision, restlessness, fatigue, agitation, a tightness in your stomach, stomachaches, poor digestion, and poor sleep and cell regeneration, leaving you feeling strung out and exhausted.[1-9]

The consequences at the emotional level that you may experience are a loss of control, anger, rage, a relentless feeling of dread, hopelessness, overwhelm, depression, lack of confidence and self-esteem, being on edge, impatience, a somber mood, a feeling that you might do something inappropriate, a desire to hurt, a craving or dependency, or a need to have some drama in your life.[1-9]

The consequences at the cognitive level are where your thoughts generate worry and anxiety that relate to some future event, or something that might (or might not) actually happen at some (imagined) point in the future; that something awful might happen to you or one of your loved ones; those "what if," or "when I," or "I am not good enough," fear-based thoughts.[9]

Real life personal experiences

I myself have for many years experienced such consequences first-hand.

For example, my worry and anxiety took a decisive grip over me and triggered my medically diagnosed IBS when I had to make a key presentation to a large number of my professional peers.

I was laid up in bed for four days, exhausted, dripping with sweat, feeling nauseous, and I would cycle between bouts of diarrhea (on one day) followed by constipation and bloating (the next day).

Yes, not a very pretty picture, but at least I managed to avoid the danger of slipping into a crippling state of depression, or potential self-harming, or some other serious long-term health problem or issue.

There were many occasions when all the noise and chatter of my mind, created from being in a constant state of worry and anxiety, would result in me missing some vital piece of information that I needed to know to complete some important or essential task.

I would then spend an age *beating myself up* mentally, for not paying attention and for having to suffer the consequences of not being able to do the important, or essential, task at the right time.

So I know exactly what it is like to suffer from those intrusive and disruptive thoughts and emotions that lead you to overwhelm, exhaustion, anger, rage, panic attacks or depression, and self-harm or substance abuse, although fortunately through sheer determination I managed to avoid most of the consequences of the latter.

To be clear, this book reviews the actual causes of your worry and anxiety and the principal options available to you to stop (or to *"banish"*) your worry and anxiety, and looks at why you might resist doing this (and deny yourself the above benefits).

This book is not just another review of the latest psychology research studies into worry and anxiety.

The LENSE+GP method

You won't need a psychology degree, or to understand the many complex psychological terms and concepts that have been researched, in order to make full use of the LENSE+GP method.

In fact, if your only interest is in trying out the LENSE+GP method for yourself, you can, if you wish, simply go straight to that chapter.

Alternatively, you may prefer to read all of the chapters, to gain a deeper understanding of the probable cause of your worry and anxiety, and of all the 5 brilliant ways to stop that actually work.

As always, that is entirely your choice.

Wherever possible, the relevant references are provided to the research studies used in this book and upon which the LENSE+GP method is based.

You therefore have full access to the source material and content, so that you can do your own due diligence regarding any potential technique that you may think is appropriate to you and to your unique circumstances or situation.

In research terms, anxiety is generally considered to be a more disruptive and problematic psychological state than worry; however, worry is usually considered to be a mild form of anxiety, and if not recognized and effectively managed, it could easily drag you into the more advanced stages of anxiety.

Therefore, throughout this book we use the terms interchangeably and collectively, rather than attempting to constantly separate out all of the various components individually.

This book is based upon the author's real-life experiences and over two years of research and development, of trial and error, in order to create a simple, easy-to-use, and almost effort-free system, that actually works, and that takes less than 30 minutes in total a day to achieve and maintain.

The many benefits of the LENSE+GP method

This is the same simple and easy-to-use system that I myself still use every single day.

This method is purposely designed to be *simple, easy, and almost effortless to use* and provides you with a known, predictable, and consistent outcome, and the more you use it the better your results.

In this book you will also discover the most helpful secret (that is hidden "in plain sight") that a near-death experience in Malaysia taught me.

We also explore and answer the question: if you suffer from worry and anxiety, will your children also suffer? And if so, is there anything you can do about it? You might be surprised at the answer!

The book is provided solely for the purposes of enabling you to experience for yourself the benefits that can come from a system that is known to work to provide you with a worry- and anxiety-free state of mind, without you having to undertake all of the research, testing and development, time and effort (and cost) that it would otherwise take you to achieve a similar system.

For a long time during my research, I also struggled to fully understand the concept of what some researchers and psychologists refer to as the "false self," and the role that this plays in your worry and anxiety.

Until, that is, one day I found myself asking this question – and you might have asked the same question:

Who is it that is listening to your thoughts, to the little voice in your head and the constant chatter and noise in your mind, if this is not you – the real you – your true self, the one that is listening and observing the thoughts that create your feelings and emotions, and therefore worry and anxiety?

As you will discover (amongst many other things) in this book, you are not your thoughts, the person that you perhaps think you are, or that you identify yourself with.

You will discover, in later chapters, that your mind is an accumulation of impressions or thoughts, and with the information and help provided you will come to realize that these impressions are not you.

Interestingly, research studies[48] show that when you attempt to suppress your thoughts, you *actually increase the frequency of those very same thoughts*, creating the very opposite effect, or outcome, to that which you wanted or intended (to banish your worry and anxiety).

No wonder it is so hard to stop your worry and anxiety.

As I have already said, I am just a regular guy and in no way special, and for me, my consistent daily practice of the LENSE+GP method has created some amazing benefits.

It has changed forever my beliefs, thinking, feelings and emotions, and finally allowed me to enjoy a worry and anxiety free state of mind, and my hope is that it will do the same for you.

You then, like me, will only need to don your headphones, relax, hit the play button on your MP3 player, and simply listen during your scheduled daily time slot to get to enjoy the amazing benefits that only a worry and anxiety free state of mind can give you.

So just imagine, if you dare, how it would feel for you to finally escape the pain and suffering from the negative physiological, emotional, cognitive, and behavioral consequences to your health and wellbeing.

To escape those intrusive and disruptive thoughts and emotions that lead you to overwhelm, exhaustion, anger, rage, and the feeling of hopelessness and deep dread of having to face yet another day of difficult conversations, of panic attacks or depression, or even self-harm or substance abuse.

And instead to experience the sheer bliss of being free of all your worry and anxiety, to wake up fully refreshed, with a clarity of mind that lets you focus on what really matters to you the most.

To be finally free from all the constant noise and chatter in your mind, free of all of those "what if" fear-based thoughts, to finally have a clear and focused mind that is ready to serve you! Image how that feels!

Read on and enjoy…!

The Significant Consequences of Your Worry and Anxiety

Chapter 1

The Significant Consequences of Your Worry and Anxiety

Probably, at some time or other, you have been told, or you may have heard someone say, that you should *stop all of your worrying, it is not good for you,* or that *nothing helpful or good ever came from worrying,* or that *all that worry will make you ill.*

Even though you probably agree with them, it simply does not help you to know this.

So you simply continue to go about your life as usual, regardless of the very real and significant consequences that your constant worry and anxiety have with regard to your long-term health and wellbeing.

Perhaps you have never seen your worry and anxiety to be anything other than an annoyance, or just a bit troublesome.

This overlooks the ever-growing weight of scientific research material and evidence, which now clearly shows that worry and anxiety have very real and significant life-threatening consequences to your health and wellbeing.

These real consequences of your worry and anxiety can manifest themselves in many different ways and in different forms, and to many different levels of severity, and this can be different for each of us, as we are, after all, unique.

According to researchers at the renowned Harvard Medical School, worry is a component of anxiety, and anxiety has three interrelated components[2] – physiological, emotional, and cognitive – to which is usually added a fourth component, the behavioral component.

You may experience one or more of these interrelated components of worry and anxiety at different times in your life, or at any time of your life, or in some severe cases almost all of the time (some of us are 'born worriers' after all…)

Some low level of worry and anxiety is of course both necessary and required to ensure your safety and to motivate you.

It is, after all, what provides you with that extra energy you need to improve your focus and attention in order to complete that important or critical task that you have to do.

You probably already know that your worry and anxiety will automatically, and subconsciously, trigger part of your limbic system (a neural network) known as the amygdala part of your brain, which then sends signals to your hypothalamus.

Your hypothalamus activates your sympathetic nervous system, releasing various hormones and chemicals (from your adrenal glands) as part of what is generally referred to as the "freeze, fight, or flight" response.

This primeval part of your auto-response system automatically controls your involuntary body functions, such as increasing your breathing, blood pressure, and heartrate, and diverts your blood flow away from your stomach area to your brain, preparing you for the anticipated freeze–fight–flight action response.[1,3]

This response typically results in you becoming dizzy and lightheaded, with you losing the ability to focus, feeling sick, and experiencing a stomachache or diarrhea.[1]

This process is part of our inherited ancestral way of life, where to survive a sudden ambush from a tiger-toothed mammal or unfriendly rival tribe, we had to instantly and automatically, and without any hesitation or delay, respond by taking the required action to avoid being mauled or injured, or killed and eaten.

Studies[3,4] have shown that, when this response becomes a frequent event, it will over time have serious consequences to your long-term health and wellbeing.

Having such a response frequently will establish a dominant neural pathway that will further increase the reoccurrence of the response.

Consequences for you of the *physiological component*

The consequences to you of the *physiological component* of your worry and anxiety might be experienced (at the low end of the spectrum) as tension or aching in your muscles, as clammy hands and excessive body sweating, as heart palpitations, breathlessness, dizziness, and headaches.[1,9]

And when it comes to that time of day when you should be going to sleep, you might simply not be able to quieten your mind sufficiently to enable you to fall asleep, and when you eventually do so, you will often wake up in the middle of the night and then struggle to get back to sleep again.

Your poor sleep interferes with your body's and brain's ability to rest and repair itself (regeneration of cells), and this leaves you feeling strung out, fatigued and exhausted, agitated and restlessness, irritable and moody, creating all kinds of relationship issues for you at home and at work.

You simply don't seem to have any energy to do anything and you may even be unable, or unwilling, to get out of bed (you think, *Why bother, what is the point anyway?*) unless you are forced to do so.

You are not able to concentrate or focus or to pay sufficient attention to the task that needs to be done, or to do it in an effective and efficient manner, creating indecision and procrastination, all of which lowers your self-esteem and overall sense of worth.

Research studies[1,7,8,15] have shown that worry and anxiety are linked to poor digestion and to stomachaches and general digestive disorders such as Irritable Bowel Syndrome (IBS), with its associated bloating and cycles of diarrhea and constipation.

At the higher end of the physiological component spectrum, research studies[38] have shown that worry and anxiety can result in chronic illnesses such as respiratory disorders, including cardiovascular disease and other chronic health conditions, resulting in a *significant reduction in your life expectancy.*[1,5]

Two further studies[1,5] found that you are twice as likely to suffer a heart attack if you suffer from anxiety than if you don't – yes, you read that correctly, and just think about that for a moment – you are *twice as likely to suffer a heart attack* (59% in women).

Consequences for you of the *emotional component*

The consequences (at the low end of the spectrum) of the *emotional component* of your worry and anxiety may leave you feeling that everything and everyone represents a serious challenge to you, even more so when the *physiological component* may already have left you feeling lethargic and physically run down.[1,3,9]

This will understandably make you irritable, and should you, for instance, finally manage to force yourself to get out of bed, you will wonder why you have bothered to do so, since you feel that nobody really cares about you anyway, and everything and everyone just seems to annoy and irritate you.

When you go about your daily tasks it is as if you are on autopilot, without you actually being there, or being properly engaged in the task at hand, or making any meaningful contribution.

All of which simply eats away at your self-esteem, lowering your degree of self-confidence even further.

You will often feel on edge and will self-criticize, and you constantly ask yourself, "What is wrong with me?" as you become more and more aware that you are not in control of your moods and feelings.[6]

You blame yourself for not being able to control your emotions and feelings, for your constant irritation, your anger and rage, your impatience and regular mood swings. Your thoughts cause you to be tense and upset, and you don't understand the reasons why.

If you commute to work, you find that the slightest incident results in you becoming more and more irritable, and you become more and more annoyed and angry. It is as if the world is against you.

Having to wait, for example at traffic lights, or in line at the checkout, just incenses you even more, and you see this as yet more proof that the world is conspiring against you.[3]

This can rapidly escalate into a significant verbal or physical confrontation, or to a feeling that you might do something inappropriate, like having the desire to self-harm.

Your worry and anxiety often creates within you a feeling of dread, of hopelessness and of overwhelm, and you have a sense of impending doom and gloom.[9]

At the higher end of the spectrum, your worry and anxiety can trigger high levels of fear-based emotions and even terror within you, and it can do so at an alarming speed.[4]

This can quickly take a complete hold over you and can lead you toward experiencing a panic attack,[4] or perhaps developing a dependency, or a need for you to have some drama in your relationship of one kind or another.

Consequences for you of the *cognitive component*

The *cognitive component* of your worry and anxiety often results from you having thoughts that relate to some future event, something that *might* (or might *not*) actually happen to you at some (imagined) point in the future – that something awful *might* happen to you or to a loved one.

If so, then much of your thinking will be centered around the classic "what ifs" – "what if" I should become ill, or I cannot pick the kids up from school, or "what if" I fail to get to work or to a scheduled meeting on time; "what if" I have an accident, or the car should break down, or I should get lost?

Or perhaps, "what if" I don't finish this task on time? What will my boss think of me, or my co-workers or colleagues think of me? "What if" I should lose my job or my partner leaves me? How will I be able to cope or pay my bills? "What if" I get into debt… "what if"… "what if"…?[9]

You might also have thoughts based on you waiting for some future event to happen. For example, "When I get… then I will be able to…" or "If only I had…" or "If only I could win… then I will be free to… I will be happy… and all my worry and anxiety would finally cease…" Perhaps you can relate?

Alternatively, you might have reoccurring thoughts about some past experience or situation you may have had, or an interaction with someone that could have gone much better than it did.

You then relive the experience all over again in your mind in a futile effort to *make it right*, or to *make it better*, or to *put it right* (a perceived injustice), all of which just reinforces your learned or acquired belief, making it even more likely for you to experience further repetition of these unhelpful thoughts.[36]

Having such a *cognitive component* of your worry and anxiety results in you having unrealistic or unfounded fears, which creates for you an ultra-sensitivity to your environment or circumstances, where you see everything and everyone as a potential threat.[6]

You can have seemingly uncontrollable or obsessive thoughts, that anticipate the very worst possible outcome of some potential future event, or are based upon a challenging past experience, rather than you taking a more balanced view (maybe it will happen or maybe it won't happen, and if it does happen then I will deal with it when it does…).

When your mind is full of worry and anxiety, there is no room available in your mind for anything new to enter – no room for you to use it or to focus on what needs to be done, or to find a solution to a problem.[17]

You might attend a meeting, or some complex training, and your thoughts create an almost constant level of noise and chatter in your mind.

This disrupts, or interrupts, your concentration and focus to the extent that you miss the important piece of information you need to know about, or the specific point that the trainer is telling you.

You need to know this information, but you cannot go back in time and relive the moment and discover what you have missed – no matter how much you wish you could – so you dwell upon this and constantly beat yourself up about it.

When you're in bed, desperately trying to get to sleep, you are tossing and turning and telling your mind to be quiet and to stop all of its constant noise and chatter and to let you sleep,[4] so that you can rejuvenate and repair your tired body.

Instead, however, just when you seemed to be able to quieten your mind, another thought pops into your head and you find yourself experiencing even more thoughts and things to worry and be anxious about,[3] and you find you are right back to where you started.

When you wake up in the morning to what seems at first to be a small worry, as the ever-increasing demands of the day take their significant toll on your general wellbeing, this small worry becomes more and more troublesome to you and develops into a severe and debilitating type of worry and anxiety.

You are distracted by all of the negative thoughts that somehow magically *pop into your head*, and by the voice that you hear that keeps telling you that you will never get the task that you are doing done.

This creates doubt in your mind about your ability to be able to complete this task (or any task) that you need to do: you feel that the task is just too difficult for you, or is just too complex for you, or that you are not good enough, or not smart enough, all of which results in you making little or no progress in actually completing the task.

When I was first married, my spouse would wonder why I would suddenly become detached and withdraw myself into what looked to her to be a trance-like state of being. "He has 'gone' again," is what she would think and tell people who noticed.

This was actually a personal ritual of mine where I would engage in a hurried or emergency prayer, or plea, performed in my mind in a fearful and anxious state of worry and anxiety. By doing this, I would attempt to neutralize or prevent some negative thought that had suddenly and uncontrollably "popped" into my mind from actually happening or becoming a reality for me or one of my loved ones.

These types of thoughts impair your ability to focus and concentrate, or to think clearly and make decisions, to be able to function properly or effectively, or even to function at all.

They paralyze you and create procrastination where you simply cannot decide what to do, or you are not able to choose the "right" option whenever you have a choice or decision to make.[9]

The cumulative effect of today's hectic lifestyle and extreme pressure on you to perform and compete in all areas of your personal and professional life, and the need to constantly compare yourself (almost without thinking) against everyone else, including so-called celebrities (or rather the *polished* versions of them), leaves you feeling that you are inadequate and you just cannot cope.

You perhaps begin to wonder, and then to worry about, where all of this is leading you to, and you ask yourself, "What has happened to me? Why me? What is going on? I used to be so good at this... it used to be so easy!"

Your thoughts and the voices in your head tell you that you should be happy, you should be content, you should be grateful for what you have.

You become desperate to break free and escape this never-ending cycle, and you wish you had a door to walk through to be able to leave this all behind you.

You may become desperately unhappy and there is no sense of *flow*, contentment, or enjoyment anymore in anything that you do. You have a need to repeatedly check everything, or to seek assurance from others.

Consequences for you of the *behavioral component*

As we have seen, many of the physical and emotional or cognitive components of your worry and anxiety can trigger a variety of pain and suffering; therefore, and quite understandably, you will try to change or adapt your behavior and habits to avoid exposure to such situations or circumstances.

The consequences of the *behavioral component* of your worry and anxiety will therefore often be experienced by you trying to avoid these specific situations or circumstances, such as avoiding a particular location, or a large gathering of people, or large crowds, enclosed spaces, a certain type of insect or animal, or other phobias such as the fear of flying or of making a presentation.[2,9]

You may literally feel too distressed to work (or to be able to work effectively or efficiently) as you are always thinking about your coping strategies, in an effort to avoid having to deal with a given situation or circumstance (that might happen) or people.

This then impedes your ability to think rationally and productively.

This behavioral avoidance stops you from achieving the success you deserve and could otherwise achieve, prevents you from fulfilling your true potential, and ironically often makes your situation worse.

You will probably associate a situation or circumstance with a particular negative outcome or painful experience, and you have probably developed a large repertoire of excuses that enable you to avoid exposure to such situations or circumstances.

Indeed, you may have become very good at inventing such excuses, which may now come almost naturally to you.

You may seek relief from your worry and anxiety by overeating or making unhealthy food choices, or by using alcohol, by smoking, using drugs, or participating in substance abuse, or by seeking some attention (or drama) that might come from you entering into, or enduring, an unhealthy or harmful relationship.[4,9,15]

You may feel like you are being watched or that everyone is judging you, which makes you feel as though you are somehow inferior or inadequate, not helped by your need to compare yourself to others and to the so-called celebrities, who appear (to you at least) to be so good or so successful.

Your worry and anxiety can be infectious to others around you, causing those that are close to you to also worry and become anxious, and creating for them all of the same issues and concerns for their wellbeing.

Yes, your worry and anxiety really does have very serious, and long-term, negative consequences on your overall health and wellbeing, as well as your sense of self-worth and contribution, your general productivity, and those around you.

I myself have for many years experienced such consequences first-hand.

For example, the physiological and the cognitive components of my worry and anxiety took a decisive grip over me and triggered my IBS (as medically diagnosed) when I had to make a key presentation to a large number of my professional peers.

I was laid up in bed for four days, exhausted, dripping with sweat, feeling nausea, and I would cycle between bouts of diarrhea (on one day) followed by constipation and bloating the next day.

Yes, not a very pretty picture, but at least I managed to avoid slipping any further along the spectrum toward deep despair or dread, which could have so easily taken me into a crippling state of depression, or potential self-harming, or some other serious long-term health and wellbeing problem or issue, such as substance abuse.

When the consequences of one or more of the above components of your worry and anxiety interfere with the normal activities of your life, you are often clinically classified as suffering from a condition or illness referred to as generalized anxiety disorder.

According to one study,[49] it is estimated that some 27 million Americans will suffer some form of anxiety disorder during their lives, so you should realize that this is not an uncommon condition, it is not your fault, and you are most definitely not alone.

In fact, a recent report by the Anxiety and Depression Association of America suggests that figure has risen to some 40 million adults in the USA.

According to the World Health Organization in 2017, the total estimated number of people living with anxiety disorders in the world is 264 million, an increase of 14.9% since 2005.

So, as I have said, you are not alone, and it is certainly not in any way your fault.

Why You Might Resist Stopping

Chapter 2

Why You Might Resist Stopping

Perhaps you simply were not aware that your worry and anxiety was such an important and significant health and welfare issue, or you are not aware of the options available to you, to take back control of your life and start to live it the way it was intended to be lived.

Or perhaps there is something else holding you back?

From my research of the extensive published materials, it became very apparent that the pain and suffering that you create from your worry and anxiety is nearly always some form of unconscious resistance, or non-acceptance, of *"what is"* (an acceptance of things *"as they are"*).

This is most often as a result of some form of judgment (or a negative response) you have to your thoughts, and often this is at the unconscious level of your mind.

This usually results from a misalignment of the interpretation that you place on those thoughts and your (acquired or learned) beliefs and principles.

Studies[16,17] now show us that the way you think determines the way you respond to and interact with everything that happens around you.

Those responses (through the filters of your beliefs and principles) determine your emotions, and your emotions determine your actions, and your actions determine your outcomes or results.

It is probably worth your while pausing for a moment and reading those two paragraphs again.

When you read them, let it really register and sink into your consciousness, as it is all too easy just to read it and let your egoic mind tell you that you know this already, and therefore overlook, or underappreciate, or undervalue its relevance.

Perhaps, like many others, your compulsive thinking has become an addiction and gives you a false sense of identity or pleasure, pleasure that invariably turns into pain, fear, worry, and anxiety.

You know this only too well, so why is it so difficult to change?

One main reason is said[17] to be because you have become identified with your worry and anxiety, and you derive your sense of "self" from the associated activity of your mind, activities that are based upon your learned and acquired beliefs and principles.

This creates for you a belief that should you stop, your very identity, the person that you think you are, would cease to exist, and therefore if you should stop you would effectively die.

For simplicity, this mental identity (a phantom identity of your real "self") is generally referred to as your "ego," or more precisely your "egoic mind."

The term "ego" may mean different things to different people, but here it means a false self, created by the unconscious identification with the mind through your thoughts, and from those thoughts your resultant conscious and unconscious emotions.

For a long time during my research, I struggled to fully understand this concept of "false self" until one day I asked myself this question, and you might have the same question:

Who is the one that is listening to your egoic mind, to your thoughts, to the constant chatter and noise, or the little voice in your head, if this is not you – the real you – your true self, the one that is listening and observing all of your thoughts and worry and anxiety, rather than the person that you think you are (aka, your thoughts)?

Research studies[48] show that when you attempt to suppress your thoughts, you actually increase the frequency of those very same thoughts, creating the very opposite effect, or outcome, to that which you wanted or intended.

This then creates within you even higher levels of anxiety and activates your freeze–fight–flight response with even greater frequency and magnitude than before.[3]

No wonder it is so hard to stop your worry and anxiety.

Of course, your situation and life circumstances will depend upon a number of different and very unique (to you) factors, and therefore the reasons why you are resisting change will likely be different from anyone else's.

Perhaps you have had experience of (or have looked into) some of the traditional therapy treatment techniques for worry and anxiety, but found they would involve specialized and expensive treatment sessions, the results of which are often said to be variable and inconsistent.

I have myself had experience of some traditional treatment therapies, from a very highly respected and renowned specialized European clinic.

Although very expensive (think thousands of dollars), it did provide me with a coping strategy to manage my constant worry and anxiety.

While of some initial help, I found that the lengthy therapy program provided little real long-term lasting benefit, and what benefit I did gain soon faded away when I was back in the very busy corporate world environment.

This did, however, introduce me to therapy techniques such as the Mindfulness-Based Cognitive Therapy (MBCT) program, based on traditional Cognitive Behavioral Therapy (CBT).

Incidentally, MBCT is now the preferred and recommended treatment in the UK by the government's official body, known as the National Institute for Health and Care Excellence (NICE), to prevent depression in people who have had three or more bouts of depression in their past.[20]

This treatment is said to be at least as good as drugs for the treatment of clinical-level depression,[15] and it has been found by studies to reduce relapse rates by up to a staggering 50%.[10,11]

These therapy sessions also included mindful meditation as part of a Mindfulness-Based Stress Reduction (MBSR) program developed by Jon Kabat-Zinn at the University of Massachusetts Medical Centre.[16,36]

You may have tried, or thought about, using meditation, and while studies show how effective this is for reducing worry and anxiety, you may have resisted adopting or using it, for a number of reasons.

Perhaps you have found meditation ineffective, or to be problematic, since to achieve any level of success consistently takes an experienced and skilled person (aka a Zen monk) many years of dedicated practice to reach the level of experience and proficiency necessary to achieve consistent results.

If you were a Zen monk and practiced meditation for, say, four to six hours every day, for 22 years, this would equate to a total of something like 40,000 hours of practice and experience.

So perhaps, like me, you just don't have that amount of time available from your busy corporate lifestyle or hectic life to commit to practicing meditation.

Or perhaps you have found meditation to be boring, or your environment or circumstances are such that you have too many distractions or competition for your time, or you have simply tried it but it just did not work for you.

This is one of the reasons why I put so much time and effort into researching the use and effectiveness of modern technology.

I wanted to know if there were now proven solutions available that would overcome all of these problems and difficulties or limitations, and, as you will see shortly, I am so glad that I did.

When you understand the consequences and the harmful long-term health conditions that your worry and anxiety can create for you, it will probably be useful and of benefit to you to understand the root causes of these, and what options you have to improve your situation and overcome your resistance.

But first, I would like to share with you a profound "secret" lesson I learned from a near-death experience I had in Malaysia, and how this made me appreciate how other people, in a very different culture, were able to simply bypass their worry and anxiety altogether.

The Secret Coping Strategy Revealed by a Near-Death Experience

Chapter 3

The Secret Coping Strategy Revealed by a Near-Death Experience

I had to learn the hard way that no matter what you might be worried and anxious about, in reality it seldom if ever gets anywhere near as bad as the worst-case scenario playing through your mind.

Very often, regardless of your actual circumstance or life situation, your best strategy is to simply accept your circumstance or situation for "what it is" and to quieten your mind.

Let me explain!

During 2001, there were six of us senior managers working for a very large blue-chip global corporation, and we landed at Penang International Airport in Malaysia from Singapore, for some team bonding.

We took three separate limousines (or "limos") and set off for the Shangri-La's Rasa Sayang Resort and Spa, a five-star hotel on the beach on the opposite side of the island to the airport.

This was very nearly the last thing I would ever do.

The journey didn't start too well, as our corporate health and safety policy risk assessment insisted we traveled in three different vehicles (no more than two in any one vehicle), and I was traveling in the third or last limo.

The other two regular drivers had already left, and our driver was fluffing about setting and adjusting a Malaysian GPS unit. We were in the smallest car and clearly this was not a regular limo, or a regular driver, and the other two cars had by now very quickly and completely disappeared from view.

After only 30 minutes or so into the journey, we found ourselves heading up a very scenic but very steep mountain road and navigating our way around some very sharp blind bends (think Italian Alps with ~300-degree bends). It was a real mountain pass with drops that fell away at a height of at least 1,000 feet from the edge of the road, and of course there were no safety barriers.

Now in these cultures, like many Asian cultures, you need to remember that it is extremely *bad luck* to collide with or in any way injure a cow, or even worse a holy man, both of which seem to be regularly found walking down the center of the road with everything and everyone swerving to avoid them.

Now when I say *bad luck*, start thinking of a being-stoned-to-death type of *bad luck*.

Since the driver appeared to be frantic and anxious at having fallen so far behind the other two more experienced drivers, he considerably increased his speed, and my worry and anxiety got the better of me, fearing that the worst thing that could happen was about to happen.

Yes, I became fearful that we would literally drive over the edge of the mountain, or hit a cow, or a holy man, and perhaps be stoned to death.

So, I gestured to the driver that we had plenty of time, so he had no need to worry or feel anxious, nor any need to go so fast; we had after all the GPS satellite navigation. I (mistakenly and regrettably) pointed to my watch and his satellite navigation.

Now to be fair, English was not (unusually for Malaysia) the driver's first or second language, and somehow he interpreted my gestures as disappointment in losing time and contact with the others, so he increased his speed even more.

As we sped up the mountain and around the next blind 300-degree bend, we drifted out and hit the front wheel of one of those very large haulage trucks (think Tonka toy) coming down the mountain carrying a full load of granite-type rock – and, needless to say, the truck did not move from its position on its slow descent.

We literally bounced off this huge truck's front tire, and, fortunately, this sent us back across to the center of the road – but unfortunately, yes you guessed it, straight toward a sacred cow meandering down the middle of the road, closely followed by a Buddhist monk in a bright orange cloak.

As I turned and looked at my colleague (for reassurance and hope), I noticed that this six-foot-plus ex-USA Marine had his eyes firmly closed as we headed straight toward the cow and the monk.

I remember very vividly the driver shouting something that sounded like, "If it is Allah's wish…" He had one of those dangly pictures of a saint hanging from his rear-view mirror, and his eyes were firmly fixed on it rather than looking at where we were going.

I learned afterward that this was the local custom, or culture, that roughly translated means something like this: if Allah called you, no matter what you did or didn't do, you would meet your fate and your destiny; if however it was "Allah's wish" for you to be spared, then you would be spared.

This somehow seemed to transfer all of the worry and anxiety of what was a truly high-risk and anxious situation to a higher authority.

Thus it seemed to somehow enable these humble people to avoid the otherwise debilitating worry and anxiety that might otherwise engulf them and limit their entire existence or quality of life.

Anyway – and I am not entirely certain how – we managed to swerve (well, more kind of skidded in an out-of-control sort of way) and to avoid the cow and the Buddhist monk, and somehow managed to hit a motorbike (which I had not even seen), before the limo straightened and momentary came to a stop. We then sped off again.

There was a great chorus of people yelling and waving at us, and certain unrepeatable gestures (think rude or obscene gesturing).

Now, coming from a Western corporate world perspective, and with my set of life circumstances, experiences, and culture, I would rather we had attempted to put the odds of us surviving this hazardous journey in our favor by driving at a more moderate and appropriate speed, and by remaining on the correct side of the road.

There would, of course, still be some very significant and real risks to anyone traveling on this road, given the terrain, the culture, and the lifestyle of the people, the condition of the various vehicles, the state of the road, and the lack of any safety barriers, at least at the time that we were traveling.

So out of desperation, and it has to be said some panic (I had my eyes open, after all), as the driver again increased his speed, I yelled at him to slow down, and he seemed at last to understand me.

In case you are wondering, at this point my ex-USA Marine colleague had now opened his eyes, and I could not help but notice that he was now a very pale color.

When back in the relative safety and calm of our hotel rooms, I reflected deeply on this near-lifechanging journey, and what first struck me was just how very clear and sharp my mind was throughout the entire life-threatening event, and just how focused I was on everything that was happening around me.

I could, in fact, recall almost every single detail, even down to the truck's rusty front wheel nuts.

What struck me even more though (a big "aha" moment) was just how completely free my mind was of its usual constant worry and anxiety, and its usual repetitive noise and chatter. Of course, this soon returned!

My perspective and context of this journey was without doubt very different to that of our limo driver, who apparently went about the rest of his day without any further concern, worry, or anxiety.

Even the large dents in the limo didn't seem to faze or worry the driver!

This, I think, was mainly due to the difference in the culture of the local people, and in particular their apparent acceptance of "what is," or what they considered to be their destiny, as determined by the will of Allah.

To me, this was their "secret" coping strategy, which provided the local people with a way of managing an otherwise intolerable level of worry and anxiety, and the transfer of the burden of this worry and anxiety had been hidden from us "in plain sight" by what we thought of as their culture.

While it might *not* have been my (or your) custom, or culture, to simply accept things *as they are,* sometimes clearly the alternative is not at all helpful to you.

Despite my best efforts, I was very soon reliving the near-death experience over and over again in my mind, and I did so for several days.

I was also worrying and stressing myself about the potential consequences of what "might" have happened, and about what this would have meant to my loved ones back home – and of course worrying and fretting about the journey back to the airport.

Had I known about the nature and extent of this hazardous (nightmare) journey before the visit, then no doubt I would have worried about it for days and days *before* the journey.

Of course, coming from a large corporate and Western-based culture, we probably should have done a specific risk assessment and decided (for health and safety reasons…) to take the short helicopter flight to the hotel from the airport, and so travel in relative safety and style.

Then we would have been able to relax and fully enjoy this most fabulous hotel.

At the very least, I guess we should perhaps have assessed the journey more fully, regarding the current condition of the road, its risks and hazards; we should have carefully selected the limo company, assessed the qualifications and experience of their drivers, and agreed a requirement specification and contract for the limo etc. before undertaking such a journey (again) by road.

You may be wondering why I am telling you this story and what this has to do with this book.

It was this near-death experience that provided me with a valuable lesson or "secret," a profound and effective coping strategy.

The coping strategy, simply put, is that, no matter what you might be worried or anxious about, *it seldom if ever gets anywhere near as bad as the worst-case scenario playing through your mind.*

Rather than resist, or attempt to fight, the circumstances or situation that you find yourself in, most often your best strategy, and *the "secret" that was hidden in plain sight,* is *to simply accept your situation for "what it is,"* to let go of any fear-based thoughts, and to quieten your mind.

While in that hotel room, I also made a vow to myself that I would take the time and effort to discover and understand the root cause of my constant worry and anxiety, and to find a way to reduce or eliminate it, so that I could finally get to enjoy all of the many benefits that come from having a worry and anxiety free way of life… and yes, that includes fabulous five-star resorts in far-off exotic places.

I also realized that there are probably many others just like me, who are stuck in a cycle of continuous worry and anxiety that limits their performance, their effectiveness, and their ability to relax, think clearly, and focus on the task in hand.

Or perhaps to productively engage and interact with their environment or the people around them.

They too may become distracted, stressed, and racked with worry and anxiety, and suffer all of the significant negative consequences that this then has for their long-term health and wellbeing.

The 5 Principal Causes of Your Worry and Anxiety

Chapter 4

The 5 Principal Causes of Your Worry and Anxiety

Since we have already seen that your worry and anxiety can create very significant, harmful, long-term health conditions and consequences for you, it will probably be of great help to you to understand the root cause of these.

Now I know many of you will be in a rush, and you may simply skip this chapter and move straight on to the chapter on the LENSE+GP system, to get the full benefits that this can bring you.

However, for others, who want to understand what the principal causes of your worry and anxiety are, and therefore be better informed and able to understand what you can do to reduce or eliminate it, then this chapter is for you.

Principal cause 1: Your *automatic physiological response system*

Whenever you experience any perceived threat or challenge, you will automatically and subconsciously trigger a part of your limbic system (a neural network) known as the amygdala part of your brain, which then sends signals to your hypothalamus.

Your hypothalamus activates your sympathetic nervous system, releasing various hormones and chemicals within you (from your adrenal glands), in preparation of what is generally referred to as the "freeze, fight, or flight" response.[1]

This primeval part of your brain's *auto-response system* automatically controls your involuntary body functions, such as *increasing your breathing, blood pressure, and heartrate*, and diverts your blood flow away from your stomach area to your brain, preparing you for the anticipated freeze–fight–flight action response.[1,3]

This process is part of our inherited ancestral way of life and is a hardwired, built-in *automatic physiological response* to any perceived threat or challenge, in order that you could survive a sudden ambush from a tiger-toothed mammal or an unfriendly rival tribe.

Historically, this response was important as it would increase your fuel or energy reserves, to enable you to be fully primed and prepared to fight or to run away from the perceived threat or challenge.

A sprint followed by a marathon perhaps, if the threat is of course real.

This response not only occurs automatically whenever the threat or challenge is real, but also (and importantly for us) *whenever we imagine or perceive such a threat or challenge to exist* (whether it is real or not).

There is no apparent difference, to the automatic initiation of the response, between *a real threat* or challenge and one that *you imagine* to exist in your mind, from the thoughts you create from your worry and anxiety.

Your hippocampus also activates your cortices, to enable you to process large amounts of information coming from your sensory systems, or to help you solve any immediate problem you might have, and to put your experience into some form of context.[1]

However, as your anxiety and stress levels increase, these will shut down, leaving you to experience a feeling of overwhelm, or not being able to think straight, or to procrastinate[1] – a bit like your computer freezing when its processor runs out of memory.

Therefore, the thoughts that arise from your excessive or constant worry and anxiety can repeatedly trigger your freeze–fight–flight response.

This will not only automatically release hormones and chemicals into your body (such as cortisol),[3] but it will also establish (or reinforce) a neurological pathway in your brain,[41] making it much more likely for you *to repeat this response again and again.*[42]

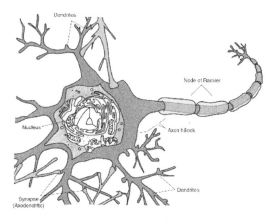

Science suggests that your brain consists of billions of connected tiny cells called neurons which form neural networks, with different networks connecting to each other by neurological pathways (NP) that can process and control information flow, so you can feel and interact with the physical world around you.[42]

They allow you to feel emotions such as anger or sensations such as hunger or thirst, and they allow you to form memories and associations and to learn new skills. [42]

As Donald Hebb put it in his landmark discovery in 1949, "neurons that fire together wire together."[42]

It is the thoughts in your mind that create your NPs, where neurons and dendrites connect in a way to represent a particular experience and associate a feeling, or an emotion, to that thought.

The more you have that thought, the larger the NP becomes and the greater the resultant emotional energy.

In turn, this increases the size of your NP, reducing its internal resistance to your emotional energy, making it a more dominant and easier-to-establish feeling or emotion. Therefore, it is much easier for you to trigger and to recall the experience.[41]

To change this feeling, or emotion, then becomes very hard for you to do, and your attempts to do so will inevitably fail – unless, and until, you establish a new thought pattern that creates a new NP that is repeated and reinforced sufficiently, and to a point where this then becomes the path of least resistance, or the new dominant NP.[42]

47

Doing this will produce a new feeling and emotion, and hence produce new actions, which will produce your new results or outcomes.

Several studies suggest, in fact, that the human brain has an amazing ability to reorganize itself, by establishing new connections between its billions of connected brain cells, to create a new NP that reflects a new belief or picture of (an imagined) reality.[41,42]

Neurologists call this remapping process *"neuroplasticity"* or *"brain plasticity."* [42]

Principal cause 2: *Acquired beliefs and conditioning*

Research studies suggest that everything you experience comes from within you, from the stimulus of the outside world through your outward-looking senses.

This is then interpreted by you based upon the filters of your learned and *acquired beliefs and conditioning* – the stories that you choose to tell yourself and the associated meaning you choose to assign to them, from which your mind then creates your perceived reality.[17]

So what exactly is this "conditioning," and what are your acquired beliefs? Glad you asked!

When we came into this world, we were very vulnerable, and by necessity we had to be cared for by those people around us. We were inquisitive and aware of everything around us with no preconceived ideas, or judgments, or beliefs, just an acceptance of our life situation or circumstance, or a total acceptance of "what is."

As a baby, you may perhaps have learned that the more and the louder you cried, or screamed, the more attention, love, and affection you received, or the more often you were fed.

As you continued to grow up, you were exposed to circumstances and experiences: to the people around you, or that you came into contact with, and their respective cultures, habits, and beliefs, and to the environment that surrounded you, be it happy, peaceful, loving, wealthy, democratic, family orientated and supportive, or domineering, full of conflict, struggle, hatred, war, poverty, famine, etc.[42]

48

Or perhaps when you were a child you were told to *do this*, or to *do that*, or *don't do this*, or *don't do that*, and when you asked *why*, you may have been told something like *it isn't right*, or *it's wrong*, or *because I say so*.

This is all *conditioning*.

You are acquiring beliefs based upon other people's perceived or learnt wisdom and their culture, beliefs, and principles or judgments, which in turn were probably passed down to them as part of their conditioning.

No matter how well intended (or not), these resulted in establishing your beliefs, principles, and conditioning, from which you interpret your particular perspective of the world.

Principal cause 3: *Fear and not being in the present moment*

Other than the very occasional real-life emergency situation that you may encounter, much of what people say, think, or do seems to be motivated by *some form of fear* that is linked to some point in their future, or their past, rather than *the present moment*.

If, for example, you are about to crash your car, then in such a life-threatening emergency situation you will shift your consciousness to the present moment almost immediately and automatically.

Your egoic mind or false self momentarily recedes and is replaced by an intense conscious presence, as was clearly demonstrated to me by my near-death experience in Malaysia.

In such a circumstance or situation, you will become calm and still but very alert, and whatever response is needed will naturally and automatically come to you.

Your action will be clear and decisive, as it arises out of your awareness while in your present moment, not as a reaction coming from the past conditioning of your mind.

It is an intuitive response to the current situation, and thus it is more likely to be effective and timely.

Anxiety, fear, worry, and panic are of course nothing new. Hippocrates wrote about anxiety in the fourth century, Søren Kierkegaard the Danish philosopher (~1813–1855) wrote about it in the mid-1800s, and Sigmund Freud did so in the 1920s.

The nature of fear, of course, materializes itself in different forms and in different ways for different people – we are, after all, unique.

The way you think therefore determines the way you respond and interact with everything that happens around you, and those responses (through the filters of your beliefs and learnt experiences) determine your feelings and emotions, and your emotions determine your actions, and your actions determine your results or outcomes.

It is therefore your thoughts that determine your emotions, your actions, and therefore your results or outcomes.

In other words, *everything begins with your thinking* – and your thoughts are therefore critical to your success and wellbeing.

How or why, then, do you have thoughts that create fear or fuel your worry and anxiety?

Due to the popularity of Eckhart Tolle's best-selling book *The Power of Now*,[17] you will probably already have an understanding and appreciation that "nothing will ever happen in the future; it will happen in the 'Now' – or, as the man himself would say:

> You have never experienced, done, thought, or felt anything outside of the present moment the Now, and you never will, as it is not possible for anything to happen, or be outside the Now. Nothing ever happened in the past; it always happens in the Now.

> What you think of as the past is a memory trace, stored in the mind [your mind], of a former Now. When you remember the past, you reactivate a memory trace – and you do so Now. The future is an imagined Now, a projection of the mind. When the future comes, it comes as the Now. When you think about the future, you do it Now
> ...

> Past and future obviously have no reality of their own ... past and future [are] only pale reflections [in your mind] ... of the eternal present. Their reality is "borrowed" from the Now.

The essence of what I am saying here cannot be understood by the [logical or conscious] mind. The moment you grasp it, there is a shift in consciousness from mind [your false self or ego] to Being [your true self], from time to presence. Suddenly, everything feels alive, radiates energy, emanates life as it really is, your true Being."[17]

The most important point for us to grasp from this is that nothing that is real exists outside of the present moment (the "Now").

If you have a preoccupation with the past, or an imagined point in the future, this will create within you fear and resistance and create a barrier to you accepting any change, which can only be accepted in the present moment (the "Now").

We will see in a later chapter how you can use this understanding and knowledge to help you remove or "banish" your worry and anxiety.

Principal cause 4: *Resistance, non-acceptance of "what is," and your egoic mind*

Research shows that worry and anxiety (and the pain and suffering that comes from it) is nearly always some form of *unconscious resistance or non-acceptance* of *"what is,"* be it some form of judgment (of your thoughts) or some form of negativity (from your beliefs, feelings, and emotions).[17]

The intensity of your worry and anxiety, and its associated pain and suffering, may largely depend on the degree of resistance you have to the present moment, and this in turn depends on how strongly you are identified with your unconscious egoic mind.

For simplicity, we may call this mental identity the "ego," or more correctly your *egoic mind*.

It consists of mind activity and conditioning and can only be kept going through constant thinking.

The term "ego" may mean different things to different people, but here it means a false self, created by your unconscious identification with the mind through your thoughts and subsequent conscious and unconscious emotions.

If for some reason you find you cannot disassociate yourself from your mind, then it is said that you have become immersed in it;[17] you are under the control and management of your egoic mind with all of its associated fear, worry, and anxiety that it creates for and within you.

You will then live almost exclusively through a situation or condition in your mind, arising from a memory trace of a past moment, or a situation or experience, or in anticipation of what the future *might* bring you, in some future imagined moment.

So, if you are in the present moment while your thoughts are in some imagined future moment in time, this creates within you an *anxiety gap*.

If you are identified with your mind, you will have lost touch with the present moment, and this *anxiety gap* will be with you constantly, *creating and fueling your fear-based worry and anxiety*.

Outside of life-threatening emergency situations or circumstances, you should always be able to cope with the present moment that you are in, but can you see that *you simply cannot cope* with something that is only a *mind projection* of an anticipated and *unreal future moment* in time?

This is probably why many people will tell you to *be careful what you wish for*, since whatever you focus your mind's attention on (your thoughts) is exactly what you will (eventually) materialize.[42]

If, for example, your worry and anxiety create thoughts that say, "I wish I could stop my constant worry and anxiety," then that is exactly what you will receive: *more wishing* you could stop your constant worry and anxiety – a self-fulfilling prophecy, perhaps at its finest![25]

Your egoic mind, of course, will try desperately to keep you in a past memory, or some imagined point in your future – as if it were telling you that you cannot get somewhere from here, because you are not yet complete, or *not good enough,* or otherwise *not sufficient* (not experienced enough, skilled enough, qualified enough, etc.).

Therefore, your logical thinking mind will tell you that *something else* needs to happen.

You need to *become this, or that,* before you can be *free* and *fulfilled,* or you need *time* to *find,* to *become,* or *to learn or understand* something, before you can finally be *free,* or before you can become *complete,* or *happy,* or *free* from *your* worry and anxiety.

You may have noticed that some people pursue very demanding physical activities of various forms, because they believe that those things will make them happy, or free them from their fear-based worry and anxiety, and in doing so they are then able to achieve some form of physiological fulfilment or gratification.

This is understood to be the search for "salvation from a state of insufficiency,"[17] and invariably it seems that any sense of achievement, or satisfaction, that is obtained is short-lived and is soon replaced by the habitual thoughts that take you again to an imaginary point into your future, and away from the present moment.

One of the reasons why some people love to engage in dangerous activities, such as climbing the world's highest mountain peaks, or high-speed car or motorcycle racing, is that it forces them into the present moment: a heightened state of being alive and free of problems, and free from the constant noise and chatter of the egoic mind, knowing that if they leave the present moment even for a second, it may mean their death.

Studies also suggest that you can become addicted to this particular type of activity, in order to relive the experience that this state of mind can provide for you.

However, I have great news for you: you don't need to climb Everest, or race Formula 1 cars, or race Motor GP motorcycles, in order to achieve this state of mind.

You can enter this state of mind anytime you wish, if you choose to do so, and if you have the right knowledge and some simple techniques, as we will see shortly.

Principal cause 5: *Your genetics*

One question that many people have is, what about genetics? Is this a cause of your high level of worry and anxiety, and if so, will any of your children also suffer the same? That's an excellent question!

So what about your genetics, your DNA: do they play any role in why you should experience high levels of worry and anxiety, and if so, what does this mean for you, and for your children?

Well, that's an interesting question. I have always believed that I inherited my constant worry and anxiety from my mother, who was a self-confessed born worrier and worried just about anything and everything.

She would jump up in a fearful start whenever there was a clap of thunder, and say, "oh god, no!"

I would say, with a smile, "It's just thunder, Mum!"

At a subconscious level this had become her learnt and acquired response, based upon her belief that something terrible was (potentially) about to happen, or *might* be about to happen.

This is easy for me to say of course, as I didn't have to live through the Blitz and the constant bombing raids of the Second World War, with the dreadful loss of life and property that this brought to many families, and to my mother's friends and neighbors.

There is a well-known experiment into genetic transfer of fear and anxiety using mice, in a study published by the Howard Hughes Medical Institute, led by Brian Dias of Emory University School of Medicine in Atlanta.[18]

In the study, two-month-old inexperienced and odor-naive male mice were subject to a substance called acetophenone, which gives off an odor like cherry blossom, and then for a short period the mice received a mild electric shock to their feet at the same time the odor was present.

The mice exhibited a fearful response whenever the odor was introduced to them, regardless of whether or not the presence of an electric shock was actually there.

On examination in the laboratory, researchers found that the odorant receptors in the mice's noses had become changed by the exposure and experience to their fear response.

The mice were left for 10 days without any odor and then allowed to mate with naive females.

The offspring of the mice were then subject to the same odor.

They exhibited the same fearful response as their parents, even though they had never encountered the odor before and were not with or under the parents influence (i.e. this was a new experience to them).

They were also found to have the same changed odorant receptors in their nose.

The transfer of DNA from the original mice to the offspring was believed to have been made via the sperm of the original males.

This experiment was repeated again, exactly as previously, for a further generation of mice, and it was found to provide the exact same fear and anxiety response, and the same results.

Another study into children of the survivors of the Holocaust[19] found evidence that trauma had been genetically transferred to them from their parents, and although there appears to be some skepticism in this particular case from some scientific groups, it is generally considered to have a valid conclusion.

In summary, then, it appears that genetics can have a role to play in you inheriting and experiencing an elevated level of worry and anxiety if your parents also suffered from this.

Scientists call this genetic transfer *epigenetic inheritance*... so thanks, Mum!

So, if you are wondering, or worrying, about whether your worry and anxiety will mean that your children will also suffer. then the answer seems to be yes.

However, there is some good news: you can now control or eliminate ("banish") your worry and anxiety, *even if this is from epigenetic inheritance*, using the new science- and technology-based proven LENSE+GP method. I am living proof of that.

The 5 Brilliant Ways to Stop – That Actually Work

Chapter 5

The 5 Brilliant Ways to Stop – That Actually Work

Now that you have an understanding of the cause of your worry and anxiety, you are in a much better position to evaluate the various options available to you to reduce or eliminate ("banish") them, in a way that is most relevant to your unique set of circumstances or situation.

While there are many so called *tips and tricks* available to help you, in this chapter we focus only on the evidence-based principal techniques and solutions that have been proven by scientific research to work, or that are from my own personal experience.

You may recall, from an earlier chapter, that I had some experience of the *traditional* treatment therapies, from a renowned, specialized European clinic.

These well-established traditional types of treatment were very expensive (think thousands of dollars).

While of some initial help – and they did provide me with a coping strategy – when the lengthy therapy program came to an end, they proved to be of little long-lasting help, and the benefits that I did get soon faded away when I was back in the very busy corporate world environment.

Brilliant way 1: *Traditional treatment therapy*

This therapy experience introduced me to some of the *classical* or *traditional treatment therapies* that are still relevant today.

Such treatments include Mindfulness-Based Cognitive Therapy (MBCT), a therapy based on traditional Cognitive Behavioral Therapy (CBT) methods, with the addition of mindfulness and mindfulness meditation.[10,12,37]

Like CBT, MBCT is based on the theory that you inevitably and automatically return to your repetitive thoughts (from your constant worry and anxiety). MBCT helps you to interrupt those repetitive thoughts.

It teaches you to not react to your thoughts but instead to simply observe and accept them without judgment.[12]

MBCT is becoming more and more recognized by healthcare providers. It is now the preferred and recommended treatment in the UK, by the government's official body (known as the National Institute for Health and Care Excellence, or NICE), to prevent depression in people who have had three or more bouts of depression.[20]

This treatment is also said to be *at least as good as drugs* for the treatment of clinical-level depression[10,15] and has been found by studies to reduce relapse rates by up to a staggering 50%.[10,11]

The therapy sessions included mindful meditation, as part of a Mindfulness Based Stress Reduction ("MBSR") program originally developed by Jon Kabat-Zinn at the University of Massachusetts Medical Centre.[16]

In published interviews, Jon Kabat-Zinn explains that mindfulness activates parts of your brain that aren't normally activated when you are mindlessly running on autopilot, in your habitual life.

You can capture these activated parts of your brain with simple practices, in a way that can be scientifically demonstrated to benefit you in many different ways.[16]

Although MBSR may have its roots in spiritual teachings, it is free from any association with religious cultures and teachings and thus has a wider appeal to western cultures.

For many years, mystics such as the Indian spiritual guru Sadhguru Jaggi Vasudev have told us:

> *When your physical body, your mind, your emotions and your fundamental life energy [your vibration levels] are all organized and synchronized in one direction, for a certain period of time, everything will become easy for you.*
>
> *You cannot allow your mind to travel in all directions as it is like trying to travel somewhere new and far away, and you keep changing your direction, the chances of you ever getting to your correct destination is very remote, and if you do so at all, it will be by chance alone.*[29]

A systematic review by the University of Surrey[38] into the available treatments to reduce worry (and rumination) found MBCT to be *effective in the reduction of worry* (and rumination) in both *internet-delivered* and *face-to-face* formats.

A separate, later, two-stage meta-analytic structural equation modelling study[36] found strong and consistent evidence that MBSR and MBCT *were especially effective strategies to stop worry.*

Mindfulness, just on its own, helps you to put some space between you and your reactions, and to break down your conditioned and learnt (habitual) responses and your environmental conditioning.[15]

The benefits of mindfulness

The research studies show that mindfulness can provide you with many benefits, such as helping you to become fully aware of the present moment, producing better engagement with your day-to-day life, and allowing you to build better connections and interactions with those around you, to reduce or eliminate levels of stress, worry, and anxiety, and even to improve your ability to sleep.[15]

While many case studies show mindfulness to improve mental health conditions such as depression,[10,11] if depression or any other mental health condition is an issue for you, you must seek advice from an appropriate professionally qualified, licensed, and registered medical practitioner.

What is mindfulness?

According to Wikipedia at the time of writing:

> Mindfulness is the psychological process of bringing one's attention to the internal and external experiences occurring in the present moment, which can be developed through the practice of meditation, and other training.

> It is a significant element of some Buddhist traditions. The recent popularity of mindfulness in the west is generally considered to have been initiated by Jon Kabat-Zinn.[16]

Mindfulness itself is about being in a state of awareness and of being fully in the present moment rather than in some projected point in an imagined future, or of a memory trace from your past.

It's about becoming aware of and observing your thoughts and feelings, accepting them without any criticism or judgment, without you engaging or resisting or feeling challenged by them, or in any way reacting to them, and it's about being compassionate with yourself.[13,15,16]

You come to the profound understanding that your thoughts and feelings (including any negative ones) are transient – just like small, fluffy, white clouds hurriedly crossing a large, clear blue sky, they appear to come and go.

Ultimately it's your choice whether you choose to act on them or not (although obviously it helps if you have a proven way to control your thoughts). More about this shortly.

Scientific studies show that mindfulness can positively modify your brainwave patterns that would otherwise drive or support your day-to-day worry, your anxiety, stress, and irritability, and modify them in a way that you are able to let go and dissipate them, with relative ease and little effort.[26,28,31]

Studies have also shown that those who regularly practice mindfulness meditation see that their memory improves and their clarity of mind, concentration, focus, and creativity all increase, while their reaction times become faster.[34,35]

Professor Mark Williams, a former director of the Oxford Mindfulness Centre in the UK, says:

> *Mindfulness means knowing directly what is going on inside and outside ourselves, moment by moment … It's easy to lose touch with the way our bodies are feeling and to end up living "in our heads" – caught up in our thoughts without stopping to notice how those thoughts are driving our emotions and behavior.*

As we have already seen, these emotions will, of course, in turn create your actions, and your actions will create your results and therefore your life circumstances or situation.

A practical application of MBCT that you can use

MBCT is noted for developing what is called the "**ABC**" model of behavior, one version of which takes an **A**ctivating Event (an event or experience that sets off the event or reaction), **B**eliefs (you evaluate what you have experienced), and **C**onsequences (what happens in your emotions, or the resultant action that you take).

The ABC model is considered as a key component of MBCT, as it suggests that your emotions or feelings are consequences of a situation, *plus the interpretation you place upon it,* and that in turn results in your emotional response or distress.

For example, perhaps you find yourself screaming at your spouse or work colleague but you have absolutely no idea why.

In other words, you have a situation of (A) and as a result the feeling of (C), but you do not recognize that your belief and conditioning system (which leads to our emotions and feelings) is responsible for connecting (A) and (C) (where (C) is you screaming at your spouse or work colleague).

These are your automatic emotional responses, which occur because we have a running commentary, a constant and repetitive stream of thoughts, that we barely notice (if at all).

These thoughts lead to your emotional feelings, and these lead you to your actions, which lead to your results and to your situation or circumstances.

By way of a practical example, let's consider a situation (A), where perhaps you happen to notice a very close friend while you are out and about shopping; they are with some other people and appear not to notice you, or to just simply ignore you.

So you might think deep down (based upon your belief system and your conditioning) that (B) they don't really like you, in fact they probably really despise you, or they think you are not good enough to be acknowledged in front of their important friends or acquaintances.

As a result (C) you are depressed or deeply hurt and saddened, and then you ruminate and worry and become anxious.

While in this low state of self-esteem, your boss then asks you to do something you don't really like doing, or don't want to do, or asks you to correct something you have previously done (in reality a small, simple adjustment), which you take to heart and interpret as proof that no-one really likes or respects you.

So by the time you next bump into your close friend, you hardly hear them saying that they are *so sorry* for not speaking to you the other day, when they were out with their new boss, as things were not going too well for them at the time, and they had to concentrate fully on what was being said to them by their new boss.

That's right, *you don't hear them say this* – and to make matters even worse, you are so consumed with your own emotions and feelings that you don't even think to ask your friend how things worked out for them with their new boss.

This in all probability creates a considerable degree of awkwardness (and resentment) from your friend toward you, which further reinforces your (misplaced) belief that no one really likes or respects you, and creates for you the negative result, or circumstances, in (C).

This example underlines the usefulness of mindfulness, which involves simply paying attention to and observing without judgment, or engagement, whatever is happening to you at that moment.

If you should find that you are criticizing yourself, then observe the criticism and just watch the activity of your judging mind, and be there as the *"silent witness."*

Simply allow anything and everything that you experience from moment to moment to simply be there *(because it already is)* and just let it be *"as it is."*

Some therapy treatment clinics, like the one I experienced, use what are called "Mind over Mood" templates.

This is where you record the situation you experience (the who, what, when, and where) in one column on the template, your corresponding mood (what you felt and a rating factor for it between 0% and 100%) in the second column, and your corresponding thought in a third column (what was going through your mind, your thoughts, images).

All of this was to learn and understand the relationship and reoccurring nature of your thoughts, your feelings and emotions (moods), and your situation – effectively, your actions and the outcome or result.

This useful process can provide you with insights into the specific nature of your thoughts that might otherwise remain hidden or go unrecognized.

Another helpful practical application

Another technique is to use what is called the "three-minute breathing space," intended to bring a mindfulness practice into everyday moments of your life.

You simply take about one minute to perform each of the following three steps:

Step (1) – *Becoming aware* of your inner experience, by asking yourself what your *experience* is right now, in this present moment, and what *thoughts* are running through your mind. Then acknowledge these thoughts and see what *emotional feelings* you have from them, and then quickly *scan your body* for any sensations of tightness, or contractions, that may be present.

Step (2) – *Gathering*, where you *redirect* your *focused attention* to your *breath*, moving into the breath itself as you expand into your abdomen area on your inhalation, and following the collapsing of your abdomen as you exhale. Every time your mind drifts away, just bring it back to your breathing.

Step (3) – *Expanding* your awareness out from your *breathing* to include the *whole of your body,* noting if any part of your body is uncomfortable or in tension or contraction. If it is, then bring your *awareness* into each of these in turn by breathing into the area, and then as you exhale, you exhale from the sensations in these areas, gently reducing the level of intensity of the sensations.

You should then take this expanded level of awareness, the reduced level of discomfort, the increased calmness and relaxation, into the rest of your day's activities.

Brilliant way 2: *Meditation*

Firstly it might be helpful to understand what exactly meditation is.

Meditation comes partly from the Latin word *meditari,* which in translation means to think, engage in contemplation or reflection, or to ponder and focus your thoughts on *something,* and partly from the Latin word *mederi,* which means to heal.

Combining the meaning of both of these Latin words and summarizing the result, it can be said that meditation is simply to *think and heal.* It is said to give practitioners of meditation the opportunity to develop a sense of calmness, connection, and fulfilment in their lives.

Patanjali, thought to be the first man in the world to write about meditation and often referred to as the scientist of the religious world, said of meditation that it is almost like a dreamless sleep, but with one significant difference: when you are in a dreamless sleep you are not aware, whereas in meditation you are aware.

Meditation can also mean just putting the mind aside and to simply watch and observe, so that it no longer interferes with the true reality. You can then see things as they are and not as your mind's interpretation and perspective of reality, which has been filtered and adjusted by your mind.

What are the benefits of meditation?

Meditation is very similar and has many similar benefits to mindfulness. It is a way of escaping and removing yourself from your conditioning and life circumstances, and from the many repetitive and reoccurring thoughts you may have.

Meditation has been shown to enhance your brain function and increase your grey matter in areas of the brain associated with self-awareness, empathy, self-control, and attention.[32,34,35] It soothes the parts of the brain that produce your stress hormones and builds those areas that lift mood and promote learning.[38]

Meditation has been found to reduce the thinning of certain areas of the brain that naturally occurs with ageing and to help you to let go of your worry and anxiety.[36]

As we have already noted from earlier chapters, there are many physical benefits to be gained from meditation, such as lowering your blood pressure and alleviating tension in your muscles.

Meditation as a spiritual practice has of course been around for thousands of years. However, it is only over the last few decades that it has become popular in the western world, where it has begun to be appreciated for all of its benefits, following significant advances in scientific technologies that provide substantive evidence of those benefits.

From the many research studies already looked at, and many more similar studies, it is now generally accepted that regular meditation (just by itself) can be highly beneficial for your physical and mental wellbeing, and that it results in a positive experience for almost everyone.

When we *combine mindfulness with meditation*, the benefits can become *dramatically more significant*, as evidenced by the many successful research studies into MBCT already referenced.

However, you still need to *overcome the many obstacles and resistances* that we looked at in an earlier chapter, before you can *consistently and effortlessly gain the benefits* from a mindful meditation.

You may not be surprised to learn that modern technology can play a very major role in overcoming the many obstacles you might otherwise encounter, as we will see very shortly.

Finding time for meditation

The secret to fitting a mindfulness meditation into your busy lifestyle is to prioritize and schedule it.

Try waking up a few minutes earlier than normal and meditating as soon as you wake up, or just before or just after breakfast. This is a good time to meditate as you won't then have to try to *fit it in* during the rest of your day.

You can practice mindfulness anywhere, but it can be especially helpful for you to set aside a regular time.

If not first thing in the morning, then perhaps do it during your morning commute to work (if you use public transport, have ear or headphones and please don't put yourself or anyone else at any risk).

Alternatively, you can meditate during your lunch break (if you are at work), or just find a quiet area where you can meditate.

Take a walk to your favorite place in the park, or by the river, or at home in the garden, or just close your eyes, listen to the sounds in your neighborhood, and breathe in the aromas around you (not car fumes, obviously!).

For best and long-lasting results, choose and schedule a time of your day in which you can become fully aware of the sensations created by the world around you.

Always try to maintain a regular and consistent time of the day in which you decide to engage in a more formal or focused mindfulness meditation program or session.

Scheduling your mindfulness meditation into your daily routine creates an uplifting mood for you to benefit from for the rest of your busy day.

Create a scheduled reminder for yourself on your phone, or in your calendar, and schedule it as you would any other life-enhancing and career-enhancing benefit, as it is easy to forget or otherwise put it off, particularly if you have a mindset of *I will just fit it in when I can.*

	Monday	Tuesday	Wednesday	Thursday	Friday	Saturday	Sunday
06:00							
06:30	LENSE method	LENSE method	LENSE method	LENSE method	LENSE method	LENSE method	LENSE method
07:00							
21:00							
21:30	Gratitude Process	Gratitude Process	Gratitude Process	Gratitude Process	Gratitude Process	Gratitude Process	Gratitude Process
22:00							

Figure 1: Simply schedule your mindfulness meditation into your daily routine

If none of these options work for you, perhaps you can take 20 minutes in the evening, or before going to bed. This is an excellent alternative, particularly if you struggle with sleep issues, as it will help to put you into a relaxed and calm state of mind and let you drift off to sleep feeling totally relaxed.

You may have tried, or thought about, using meditation, and while studies show how effective this is for reducing worry and anxiety, you may have resisted using it, for a number of reasons.

Many people will still find meditation ineffective or problematic, since to achieve any level of success consistently would take an experienced and skilled person (aka a Zen monk) many years of dedicated practice, to reach the level of experience and proficiency necessary to achieve consistent results.

Incidentally, if you were a Zen monk and practiced meditation for, say, four to six hours every day, for 22 years, this would equate to a staggering total of 40,000 hours of practice and experience.

If you are new to meditation, you may be wondering how to get started. If so, for you there is a fully detailed beginner's guide to a traditional style of meditation that incorporates progressive muscle relaxation techniques, and this can be found in the Appendix.

Dr. Edmund Jacobson in the 1930s studied and refined progressive muscle relaxation techniques as a useful aid to *reduce patients' anxiety levels*, to help them overcome their fatigue issues, and to help them to think more rationally.[56,57]

However, you may prefer the much easier option to help overcome your obstacles, challenges, and resistance to meditation, and therefore assist you in realizing the many known benefits that can be achieved with a mind that is free from worry and anxiety and is clearly focused and relaxed.

If so, then just download the highly specialized and completely FREE brainwave-enhanced Zen12 guided meditation track from the website at:

https://www.zen12.com/gift/a/thebestyou

You can then just put your headphones (or earphones) on, get yourself comfortable in your preferred location and position, press play, and drift into a deeply relaxing meditation.

Just let modern technology help you in a way that has never before been available… and get all of the benefits that only a mindfulness meditation can provide you.

Brilliant way 3: *Accept the worry, accept "what is," and then move on*

Worrying about your worries is a dangerous cycle to fall into. A 2005 study by the University of Wisconsin-Milwaukee reported that "those who naturally suppress personally relevant intrusive thoughts [engage with them] … are more distressed by … the thoughts, while those who are naturally more accepting of their intrusive thoughts are less obsessional … and are less anxious."[48]

As I alluded to earlier in my near-death experience in Malaysia, in some parts of the world the culture is very different from western culture, in respect of the level and degree of worry and anxiety we are willing to subject ourselves to!

For many of us in our western cultures, a very common *perception* of our reality is that life may not be happening the way *we think that it should happen.*

During the extensive research it was noticed on many occasions that the Buddhist philosophy teaches you that *"the root of all suffering is attachment,"* and that in order to avoid such suffering you just need to *simply accept "what is."*

So *"accept what is"* and become the *"silent witness"* and observe your thoughts about the problems and troublesome situations that would historically create worry and anxiety for you.

By *observing* them and *not engaging in them*, you are effectively making yourself transparent to them and allowing them to pass right through you, without them creating within you any negative, or unhelpful, thoughts or judgments that would otherwise perpetuate your negative feelings.

These feelings will lead you to your negative or harmful (sabotaging) emotions, which can lead you to your unhelpful actions, and then to your undesirable or unhelpful results.

To *"accept what is"* will often result in you no longer becoming annoyed, angry, resentful, concerned, or filled with avoidable worry and anxiety.

This is because you are remaining in the present moment rather than some imagined future moment created by your *egoic mind, or false self*, or a memory trace from a past experience.

Brilliant way 4: *Stay in the present moment*

Ask yourself, what *"problem"* do you have right now – not next year, tomorrow, or five minutes or ten minutes from now, but what is wrong with this precise moment?

As we have already discovered, you can always cope with the present moment, but you can never cope with some point in your imagined future – nor do you have to – as the answer and the right action and the right resource will be there for you when you need it, not before and not after.[17]

Here is a simple, practical test you can easily try for yourself to see if you are in the present moment. Ask yourself: is there engagement, a sense of joy, ease, and an effortlessness in whatever it is that you are doing? If not, then you are almost certainly not in the present moment.

And if you are not, you will most likely perceive your life to be a struggle, unless and until you give your fullest attention to whatever the present moment presents to you, and you accept what your current life situation or circumstances are *(accept what is),* because you cannot give your full attention to something and *at the same time resist it.*

As we have already determined, the *present moment* is a very important place, as it is *the only place you can affect your future.*

You cannot create your future in the future; you cannot create the future in your past – *you have to create it in the present moment.*

When your attention remains in the present moment you can feel a presence, a calmness, a stillness, an inner peace, an *acceptance* of *"what is."*

You are no longer dependent on the future for your salvation, and the joy of experiencing you, as *your true self,* enters into everything that you subsequently do.

You are no longer attached to your results, and therefore neither failure nor success has the power to negatively influence you or your newly found state of inner peace.

From this new experience of knowing *your true self* comes the pathway to your freedom from worry and anxiety, since these are dissolved when you are in the present moment, in the same way that shinning a light on a shadow dissolves the shadow.[25]

Simply staying in the present moment, accepting *"what is"* and just letting go of a memory trace from a past moment, or of some imaginary future moment, *creates the time and space* for you to absorb, to take on and progress the task you have in hand, or the things that matter to you the most, and for you to achieve your desired result or outcome.

Brilliant way 5: *Enter the state of "No-Mind"*

There is a simple little trick to eliminate your worry and anxiety.

Remember when we looked at the causes of your worry and anxiety: if you are not able to quieten your mind then you are not in control of it, and your egoic mind is in control of and manages you, and you cannot give your mind *a clear and consistent direction* about where you want it to go.

So how do you quieten your mind and eliminate all of the noise and (thought) chatter? Glad you asked! However, although this is going to sound so simple and easy to do, trust me, while it is simple, it is *not easy* (and I really do know…).

Here is the little *"trick"* (or *"secret technique"*) you can use to disengage, interrupt, or reset and quieten your mind, and to remove your worry and anxiety.

Simply enter into the state of *No-Mind*, or as it is referred to in the world of Zen, *"mind of no mind"* – a practical and most useful transformative state.

This simple *thought control technique*, once learned and put into practice, clears your mind of your non-helpful or non-relevant thoughts, removes all of the *clutter*, *noise*, and *chatter* of your egoic mind, provides absolute clarity and focus, and *frees you from worry and anxiety*.

You will simply be amazed how much *more effective and efficient* you *suddenly* become – it is like switching to a very powerful turbocharger on the latest high-performance car (think Ferrari or VW Veyron), and once learnt it seems *almost effortless* to do.

I first came across the concept of *No-Mind* while reading the much-acclaimed book by Andy Shaw called *Creating A Bug Free Mind*, described as *"the world's first antivirus for the human mind."*[25] I began playing around with the concept, to see if it could be incorporated into other concepts and techniques I was researching and experimenting with.

For me it is the best form of mind *interrupt* or *reset* that I have ever found.

Now before going any further, I need to point out that there are in fact what I consider to be two different versions of *No-Mind*.

While one version, for me, has shown me huge benefits without any real effort, the other version (the version known and adopted by the world of Zen whose origins are from Chan Buddhism in China) has a fundamentally different interpretation.

In the version of *No-Mind* that I prefer, and that I use every day, you seek to focus on clearing your mind of all thoughts (a true state of *No-Mind*) and then to stretch this period (that is free of all thought) further and further.

As always, it is your choice, of course, as to which version you choose to use; I suggest you simply adopt the version that intuitively feels right for you.

We will come back to the Zen version in a moment; however, there is a specific reason why I chose the version of *No-Mind* that has the absence of *all thought*.

When you combine it with simple and easy-to-use modern technology (that has been specifically selected and tested) and a mindful meditation, in a very particular way, this can become part of a very powerful and effective method to remove (banish) your worry and anxiety, as we will see very shortly.

This combination should not be dismissed lightly, for I have found that it can significantly intensify your results and provide you with huge benefits and advantages.

After a little practice and with very little effort, you can further enhance this, if you wish, and adopt some deep healing techniques; however, this is still in the research stage and for another time or book…

Note – email us if you're interested in knowing more about our research of this particular enhancement.

So how do you enter this state of "No-Mind" (non-Zen version)?

Once you are in a deeply relaxed state of meditation, with your conscious mind and conscious voice you assertively, and with concentrated focus and effort, tell your subconscious mind and the voice in your head to simply *"Stop"* and to *"Be Quiet."*

The thoughts in your mind will usually transition from being filled with constant chatter and noise into a state of *quietness*, where the noise falls away and stops, and there is *"nothing"*, or a mind *without thought* of any kind, or what is called the state of *"No-Mind."*

You are not asleep, or in a trance, but are just fully present, fully alert, and fully aware and in the present moment without any thought.

I suggest you don't *try* to do this, you just *do it*, and bring yourself into the state of *No-Mind* and silence your mind (don't overthink it).

If, like me, you find this difficult to do at first, try it again, and then again.

You may find at first you can attain and keep this state of *No-Mind* for only, say, 5 seconds, or perhaps 10 seconds, or 30 seconds, or maybe even a minute, or three minutes – it really doesn't matter (other than to exercise your conscious control over your mind).

Regardless of the actual time, you have just successfully interrupted and disrupted your worry and anxiety based thoughts, and along with them your worry and anxiety and (eventually) their negative consequences to your health and wellbeing.

Congratulations to you! You have now reset and cleared your mind, to allow you to focus on what you desire or need to do, or whatever needs to be dealt with.

You have finally regained control of your subconscious mind, the most powerful computer-like living thing on the planet, and it is now *at your full disposal* – well, for a few minutes at least.

So now let us go a little deeper into the detail of how to successfully do this.

When you decide you are going to bring in *No-Mind*, particularly for the first time, I suggest (just like you would do for your first meditation experience) that you find your favorite spot in your home or outdoors, or somewhere that is very quiet.

Ensure that there are no external distractions, and of course switch off all of the usual modern-day local distractions of email, Facebook, Twitter, Instagram, your phone, and all other distractions and notifications.

If, like me, you cannot at first achieve the state of *No-Mind*, don't worry.

This is not uncommon, or in any way your fault.

However, if you are making a conscious, focused effort to "*try,*" then STOP – relax – take a deep breath and hold it for a few seconds, and then exhale it fully, relax, and then decide to just do it (enter the state of *No-Mind*).

If you still fail to enter the state of *No-Mind* after a few further attempts, then I suggest you might try to look for any spaces that appear between your repetitive thoughts.

These may only be momentary pauses to start with, so concentrate, as if you had a hammer and were about to drive a wedge between those spaces, and then expand and stretch those spaces further and further apart, until you become conscious that there is a period where there are no thoughts, no noise or chatter – just the stillness and quietness of *No-Mind*.

You may find it useful, if this is your first attempt, to use some visualization techniques to help you with this task if you are still finding it difficult.

Try seeing yourself inside your thoughts and pushing them out with the palms of your outstretched hands, into the momentary gaps or spaces between your thoughts – just become present, in the moment, as the observant one, the *"silent witness"* of these spaces.

Why exactly are you going to all of this trouble? Because it is said that one of these *No-Mind* minutes is considered to be worth at least 20 minutes, or even more, *of deep meditation.*

I know from my own experience with this *No-Mind* technique that you can experience a *very deep level of bliss* and you will want to return to this state as often as you can – *it really can be life-changing.*

If your mind wanders off, or starts to fill with thoughts, as it inevitably will, just let them pass and leave.

Simply return your attention and focus fully onto your breath, feeling the air flowing into your nose and out through your mouth, and notice it making your chest rise and fall.

In doing this, you are using your conscious mind, which is engaged with your subconscious mind, and allowing you to access a much deeper level of relaxation, and to go deeper into the state of *No-Mind.*

Your mind is an accumulation of impressions or thoughts, and you will come to realize that these impressions are not *you* – therefore place no attachment or engagement or identification or judgment on your thoughts, just let them remain formless and your consciousness detached from your thinking.

77

This leads to an incredible sense of freedom of consciousness, which you may sometimes *see* as an image, such as a burst of light that grows ever stronger when you are able to hold and focus on its *image*.

By keeping your focused concentration and attention on this image, you will be able to maintain the state of *No-Mind* for even longer.

You will often feel this image, while in a deeply relaxed state, as energy pulsating through your entire body (or sometimes feel it as a warm, tingly sensation).

Notice that its intensity increases as you breathe into and out of it, just as if you were fanning the flames of a fire.

In this pure state of *No-Mind*, you have total mental clarity and complete absence of the egoic mind.

You are *without any of your worry and anxiety; your mind is not empty but fully present*, fully aware, and free from all of the mind's constant and repetitive *noise and chatter*.

You are in a state where all your questions and thoughts dissolve and evaporate; your egoic mind withdraws, leaving you in a state of pure existence, with only your breathing, the image of your energy, and the feeling of your pulsating heart.

You are completely immersed with the present moment, with no past or imagined future.

So, what about the Zen version of No-Mind?

In the Zen version of *No-Mind* you do not attempt to remove or empty your mind of all thought coming into your mind, but to simply observe them and (in some applications at least) label them.

Instead of finding, focusing, maintaining, and then expanding the state in which you have no thoughts, you *simply observe or label them*, then deliberately let go of every thought that arises.

You do not try and push thoughts away, or hold on to them, or engage with them, but just let them go, to run their course like small, fluffy, white clouds drifting across a blue sky.

You keep your attention on allowing your thoughts to come and go.

You can, if you wish, develop this version even further by asking yourself this simple question: Is this thought (or voice you are hearing) helping you with the task in hand that you are doing right now, at this very moment? Does it *take you toward* where you want to go or what you want to achieve?

If YES, then great – engage with the thought (or voice) further, and in doing so, encourage more of these helpful and supportive types of thoughts.

If NO, then instantly drop or dismiss and ignore the thought or the voice. Do NOT engage with it, do NOT judge it, do NOT try to resist it – simply pay no attention to it, just *observe it and let it go* (just be there as the *"silent witness"*).

This approach takes you closer and more quickly to your desired outcome and with greater clarity and focus.

On no account must you try to force your thoughts to leave, as resisting or engaging with a thought only reinforces and encourages that thought to return and become more repetitive and even stronger (through the process of reinforcement of your neurological pathway).[48]

As we have discovered earlier, what we think about most is what we will get more of.

Therefore, if you are repetitively thinking about an unwanted or unhelpful thought, guess what your clever subconscious mind will deliver for you… *yes, more of the very same unhelpful thoughts,* and (eventually) *the very thing(s) that you don't want.*

So simply ask yourself: is this thought you are noticing and observing helping you by taking you toward your desired outcome, or toward the completion of your task or goal, or is it taking you away from your desired outcome, or in any other way harming or distracting you?

In either version of No-Mind, your *clear and fully focused mind is now working more effectively* and *efficiently for you and your desired outcome* (for example, the completion of the task in hand), without all of the previous noise, chatter, or your worry and anxiety.

If you wish, after some practice and success with this technique, you can take this process a step further: ask yourself, *How do I remove (or replace) an unhelpful (negative) repetitive thought and replace it with a more helpful (positive) one?*

So, for example, let's assume you have the thought: *I can't do this, or this is just way too hard for me, or this is just too complex or complicated for me to understand, or I cannot possibly cope,* then try replacing it with: *I can do anything if I choose to do so and I decide to put my mind and attention and focus on doing it.* You get the idea!

Whichever version of *No-Mind* you choose to adopt and practice, you will want to keep going back to it once you become familiar with it.

I know in the version of *No-Mind* that I use, I was wanting to experience it again and again, for the energy and the sheer bliss of it, and the tremendous benefits that only the state of *No-Mind* can give you.

You will naturally want to build or *schedule this as a priority activity* into your busy daily life.

No-Mind does not mean of course that you cannot use your mind, but simply that your mind cannot use you, and by mastering this technique it will provide you with *freedom from your worry and anxiety.*

Freedom to enable you to take back control of your mind, and to reap the many benefits of your newly found and focused power.

A useful bonus technique

A further simple but very useful technique that may help you, for when you are worried or anxious, is to think about a pleasant image of your favorite place.

No matter if this favorite place is a beach, a mountain, a river, a walk, or a favorite spot in the park – bring this to your mind. Now link this favorite place as a scene in your mind with your deeply relaxed meditative state, and at the same time pinch your thumb and forefinger together while doing so.

You can choose to use either hand to do this.

With a little practice, whenever you find yourself in a stressful situation, or in a state of worry and anxiety, you can simply pinch your thumb and forefinger together and recall this scene (by association) and you will become more relaxed and much calmer, as your thoughts go back to your favorite place.

You can of course do this whenever you should feel the need to do so.

Is Modern Technology a Help or a Hindrance?

Chapter 6

Is Modern Technology a Help or a Hindrance?

Although modern technology can be very useful (and more of that in a moment), as research shows from Nanyang Technological University in Singapore, the Bradley University, and Professor Margaret Duffy of the University of Missouri in the United States, time on social media can cause envy, depression, worry, and anxiety, or can exasperate further your existing levels of worry and anxiety.[39]

This is particularly so within those commonly referred to as the "Millennials" (those born in the 1980s and 1990s, the so-called "Generation Y" and "Generation Z").

Researchers have found some Millennials feel exposed when they are without their smartphones and are rarely without them.

They are used as a window through which they see the world, and they get a sense of connection to people and everything that surrounds them, both locally and globally.

However, there are risks (and consequences) to your *constant need to "know,"* and to *keep "on top of,"* what everyone else is doing on social media, partly due to the fear and worry of you missing out, and partly due to the constant *need for you to compare everything and everyone.*

An example is the need to compare your relationships, your diet, physical appearance, relative beauty, wealth, lifestyle, holidays, homes, achievements, awards, children, the number of likes and number of followers on social media, etc.

Not only are comparisons made to friends, but also to a wide range of so-called celebrities.

To exasperate matters further, in some cases this generation also has often had to contend with the "exam factory," where they are forced to compare themselves against everyone else.

So, if you are one of the Millennials, then you need to understand that it is not your fault, and that you have *acquired* this high level of worry and anxiety based state of mind.

So what to do about technology that you apparently cannot live without?

Firstly, get into the habit of only checking your emails, or Facebook messages, or other notifications at a certain time (or times) of the day (unless your job is a helpdesk or support worker, of course!), perhaps at the beginning of, or at the middle of, or at the end of, your (working) day.

Ask yourself: *Why should I become a slave to someone else's agenda, to their needs or requirements?*

Would it be so very terrible (would the world really end?) if your friend didn't get a comment, or message, or a like, from you on their Facebook page for a whole hour, or two even?

You would then be able to batch-process several such items, and then let go of any worry or anxiety, or the *need to know*, until it's your next scheduled time to login!

Try to group all your emails and notifications together by priority, or by group, or by category. For example, a group for your boss, your partner or spouse, key customers or work colleagues, family, neighbors, schools and teachers or lecturers (that is six categories or colored prioritized groups), and then one more for all of the rest.

During your scheduled hour of being logged into your account, simply work through your emails and notifications, in a set order of prioritization.

Then scan over the rest for, say, no more than 10 minutes, should you find that you are running out of your scheduled (or allocated) time.

An important advantage of modern technology

Some modern technology is, nonetheless, very helpful to you.

It can dramatically reduce the significant time that it would otherwise take for you to achieve the benefits from a regular and deep meditation experience, and to achieve a very relaxed, calm *state of mind that is free from your worry and anxiety.*

This can create the same experience for you as though you were in fact a very experienced and skilled Zen monk, who may have practiced meditation for some four to six hours every day for, say, 22 years.

Wow... *that's a saving of approximately 40,000 hours of meditation practice!*

So, using this new science-based technology, you can now get *the same level of results,* and *the many benefits of an experienced and practiced Zen monk,* by simply using a modern technology program *in only 12 to 20 minutes a day.*

And you can now do this with *a predictable level of quality and consistency,* and *with a pre-determined level of outcome, chosen by you,* to *specifically align with whatever your particular requirements are.*

This, for me, is truly extraordinary... and represents a *dramatic advancement in modern technology.*

Yes, this modern technology now exists and uses new forms of advanced brainwave entrainment (BWE), as we will now explore.

What are brainwaves and why should we care?

Brainwaves appear as synchronized electrical pulses from your neurons as they communicate within their neurological pathways (NP).

Studies based upon real-time electroencephalography (EEG) measurements of brainwaves, using brain imaging techniques such as functional magnetic resonance imaging (fMRI or "scans"), mean that we now know precisely what is happening inside our brain when various brainwave states are present.[30,35]

We now know exactly what is happening when we are asleep, when we are focused, when we increase our energy, when we're happy, when we're being creative, and when we are anxious, stressed, or worried.[35]

We know the exact meditation signature frequencies that correspond to optimum brainwave frequencies conducive to a particular, or *required, state of the brain.*

Scientist and researchers now understand the effects these have on our brain *during and after meditation.*[30,33,34,35]

So what exactly are these brainwaves, I hear you say? Well, glad you asked…

There are five main frequency groups or categories of brainwaves called Beta, Alpha, Theta, Delta, and Gamma.

These brainwaves are in constant motion, and your brain produces consistent waves at all of these frequencies.

The main categories of brainwaves

Gamma state (39–100 Hz)

You are fully conscious, highly active, and in a learning state conducive to the retention of information, which is why some trainers get their audiences to jump up and down or dance in an effort to increase permanent assimilation of their training information.

Beta state (13–39 Hz)

Beta state represents an alert mind, a state where the mind is considered to be working, or thinking and processing, interpreting and analyzing. You are active with your normal level of consciousness and normal levels of concentration.

Alpha state (8–13 Hz)

A more relaxed, calm, peaceful, and grounded state of mind. You are more lucid and reflective; the hemispheres of the brain are said to be in neural integration (more balanced), and your level of consciousness appears slightly diffused or drowsy in a pre-sleep-like state.

Flashes of inspiration are often found to be at very specific frequencies, and people with a high level of focus are typically at a frequency of 13 Hz or 14 Hz, the so-called "sensorimotor rhythm."

People who are in a good mood state are typically at a 10 Hz frequency, which is associated with the release of high levels of the chemical *serotonin*. Some researchers believe that low levels of serotonin can lead to depression.

Theta state (4–8 Hz)

You are in a deeply relaxed, dreamless sleep-like state, used in hypnosis and your REM sleep. You are able to meditate to a deeper state of awareness and connect to your intuition; you are capable of solving complicated problems.

Theta is thought to be the specific brainwave that acts like a portal: it allows you to "speak" directly to your subconscious, to gain direct access to your beliefs and your habitual behavior, typically characterized by feelings of inspiration or a spiritual connection.

Delta state (0.5–4 Hz)

A deep, dreamless sleep state of consciousness that *Tibetan monks who have meditated for decades are able to reach*; an alert, wakened state with a loss of physical awareness.

Even if your lifestyle doesn't allow for the luxury of a full eight hours of sleep, a few hours of Delta waves can trick your brain into thinking it's had all the restorative sleep it needs; it is an ideal choice for when you want to access your subconscious, to get a sense of being connected with the universe.

It has been found that everything you do or say is regulated by the frequency of your brainwaves.

Scientists have discovered that certain brainwave frequencies (especially Alpha and Theta) may:

1. Relieve stress and promote a lasting and substantial reduction in anxiety states

2. Facilitate a deep physical relaxation and mental clarity

3. Increase verbal ability and also your IQ performance

4. Better synchronize the two hemispheres of the brain

5. Recall mental images and live spontaneous, imaginative, and creative thinking

6. Reduce pain, promote euphoria, and stimulate the release of endorphins.

Research studies involving fMRI scans and EEG brainwave monitoring techniques have led to a new, detailed level of understanding of the impact and effects that brainwaves have on the brain, which are summarized in Chart 1.

Name of Rhythm / Waveform	Waveform:	Typical Frequencies (Hz)	Typical Associated Activity:
Gamma (Y)		>39	Problem Solving, Fear, High Activity and Consciousness
Beta (β)		13 - 39	Awake, Alert, Active, Constant Thinking / Worry, normal consciousness and concentration
Alpha (α)		8 - 13	Relaxed, Calm, Awake but drowsiness in pre-sleep and pre-awake or lucid state
Theta (θ)		4 - 8	Deeply relaxed, deep Meditation, mental imagery, NREEM (non-REM) sleep
Delta (Δ)		0.5 - 4	Deep Dreamless sleep with loss of physical awareness.

Chart 1: Principal categories of brainwave frequencies and their associated human activities or states of consciousness.

But why does all this matter?

This *matters a great deal* because *everything you do or say* is regulated by the frequency of your brainwaves, and brainwave frequencies can actually *determine your mind and emotional state.*

In other words, *if you change your brainwave frequencies you can reproduce a particular state of your mind,* and therefore *your corresponding mood and emotion.*

Think about that for a moment… what if you *had a very precise way* to control your brainwaves and reproduce the exact frequencies required *for you to change your state of mind* to whatever state you wanted them to be?

You could go from being in a state of worry and anxiety, to a state of being calm and relaxed, to a clarity of mind free from all of your constant and repetitive thoughts, with an ability to focus and concentrate, with a connection and a sense of purpose and fulfilment in your life… *That is interesting,* I hear you say!

I know – I thought so the moment I realized *just how useful this could be.*

Particularly if I was then able to combine this with some other easy-to-use modern technology, and some other simple techniques I had already studied and experimented with (and we have already reviewed), as I will reveal and explain shortly.

How does BWE work and why is it so important?

A simple analogy of BWE would be to think of it as though you had two identical tuning forks placed next to each other.

If you then caused only one of them to vibrate at a particular frequency, the second identical tuning fork would then start to vibrate at the exact same frequency as the first one.

This is sometimes known as the *Frequency Following Response* (FFR), or *Frequency Following Potential (FFP)*, or simply *Entrainment*, and your brain appears to work in a very similar way.

In simple terms, your brain synchronizes to a frequency it is subjected to, in a similar manner to that of the second tuning fork example above.

If, therefore, you expose it to a particular and precise audio signal frequency, then your brain synchronizes itself to that same frequency.

Scientists discovered that by playing particular frequencies in one ear, and other frequencies in your other ear, you force your brain into a predetermined brainwave frequency and its associated state of mind, and this has led to the science that has become known as BWE.

In 1839, a Prussian scientist known as Heinrich Wilhelm Dove uncovered something that is now called "binaural beats." He found that by playing different frequencies in each ear, the difference between those frequencies is realized inside your head as a *perceived pulse* or *beat*, known as a *binaural beat*.

For example, if you played 400 Hz into the left ear, and 410 Hz into the right ear, *the difference of 10 Hz is what is actually experienced by the brain,* and in 1959 this became recognized as a BWE technique.

However, because binaural beats use *indirect methods* to create BWE, their effectiveness is somewhat diminished.

Although binaural beats are still widely available and used, modern digital technology tools have advanced considerably and now make it possible for *directly applied* methods of BWE to be used.

These are generally recognized as being *more effective and efficient*, particularly those known as *isochronic tones*, which use separate pulses of a single tone to recreate a particular frequency and the encouragement of BWE.

By exposing your brain to stimuli (such as an MP3 audio file) containing a specific encoded frequency, the brain synchronizes with that frequency, in a similar way that the tuning forks did.

As we have now learned, that frequency will *induce a resultant state of mind* that corresponds to that particular brainwave frequency.

You can *choose a particular mood* or brainwave state (that you want to be in) and simply bring about that mood by subjecting your brain to the frequency that creates that mood, just by simply playing a special audio track and listening via your headphones (or earphones).

So, instead of having to learn to meditate to a level of proficiency and consistency of a Zen monk, who if you remember may have practiced meditation for *something like 40,000 hours,* you can now, with a little practice, achieve the same level of deep meditation *by just putting on your headphones (or earphones) and pressing play on your MP3 player.*

This use of modern science-based technology seemed to me to be eminently preferable to spending all of those hours trying to learn and practice meditation properly and efficiently.

In any event, like many others, I simply never had the amount of time available from my corporate lifestyle to commit to practicing meditation and achieving the level of consistency required.

And I didn't know anyone else, either, who was willing or able to commit to that amount of time and effort from their hectic modern lifestyle.

From the many reviewed studies, it is clear that it is now possible for you to use BWE to easily create whatever state of mind you wish to enter into (the selected frequency), and in doing so you can achieve the many lifechanging benefits that a deep level of meditation will provide for you.

Want to see some typical results from the use of these programs? Then take a look at the following captured BWE images from the renowned "Brain Evolution System" from Inspire3 Ltd.[44]

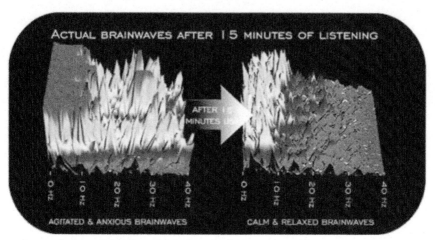

Figure 2: Sample EEG reading, showing brainwaves at the start and following 15 minutes of the Brain Evolution System program. Reprinted by kind courtesy of Inspire3 Ltd.[44]

The results above are consistent with findings of other research studies,[45] and some we have already referenced and reviewed earlier, that show the *many benefits of BWE in reducing your levels of worry and anxiety.*

In fact, one study, which used modern MRI scans, showed that even a *20-minute program*, for only four days, reduced anxiety levels by 39%.[40]

Subliminal audios

The use and effectiveness of subliminal audio tracks have been extensively researched *since the 1950s* and have been proven over many rigorous scientific studies.

Dr. Norman Dixon, a psychologist at University College London (UCL) in the United Kingdom, who provided extensive research on subliminal learning as part of his scholarly work *Preconscious Processing,* cited over

Is Modern Technology a Help or a Hindrance?

748 studies and found that over *80% of the subliminal studies delivered positive results.*[46]

So, what exactly are subliminal audio tracks?

Glad you asked!

The word *subliminal* is taken to mean *below the threshold of sensation* and simply refers to information that cannot be consciously perceived, but still has an influence.

Most practical applications of subliminal audios embed and pass subliminal messages to the mind, without the mind being consciously aware of the messaging.

They are designed in such a way as to be inaudible to your conscious mind, but audible to your unconscious mind.

Similarly, in the visual medium the messaging is designed as an image that is transmitted so briefly it is not perceived consciously, and yet it is perceived unconsciously into your mind.

Subliminal audios can *therefore bypass your conscious mind and send information directly to your unconscious mind*, and if the same subliminal messages are sent frequently enough, this reinforcement will lead to the *desired change in your habits and your belief system.*

This change comes *from within you* and is *therefore much less resisted*, or challenged, by your egoic mind, and the change generally lasts for much longer.

Studies have shown that by listening to subliminal messages in an audio track, with a precisely focused and arranged sequence of subliminal messages, you can create an intentional positive change in many (targeted) areas of your life.[47]

Changes can be made to your beliefs and habits; you can increase your motivation, boost your self-esteem, and help treat illnesses and phobias.

I have found that with careful selection and application, subliminal messages are very helpful in reducing your level of stress, worry, and anxiety.

Listening to subliminal audios is not meant to make you feel drowsy, or take you into a meditative or trance-like state.

You can usually use subliminal MP3s while you work, study, go about your daily chores, or even when exercising in the gym, or during a walk in the park or to the shops, or on your way to a meeting.

Most subliminal messaging uses the established principles of neuro-linguistic programming (NLP), which looks at the type of language we use to speak to ourselves on a particular subject, to recognize it, and then to change the language to align with that which studies have shown to be effective in creating the desired change or outcome.

Based on these principles of NLP, subliminal messaging sends suggestions to your mind that overwrite any negative or limiting beliefs that you may have acquired (through your life experiences or environmental conditioning) with more helpful, positive ones.

The simplest and most effective example of achieving this change is perhaps the use of positive affirmations.

For example, if you want to become more confident but your inner voice (your egoic mind) is saying things like, *I can't do this,* or *this will be too hard for me, or this is just too complex or too complicated for me to understand,* then the application of NLP would replace these current beliefs with a new core belief (based on someone who has abundant confidence), which typically says, *I can do anything if I choose to do so, and if I decide to put my mind and attention and focus on doing it.*

Dr. Eldon Taylor, director of Progressive Awareness Research and a Fellow in the American Psychotherapy Association, firmly believes that subliminal information, when presented in an appropriate manner, is processed, retained, and acted upon.[47]

For both my own benefit and that of readers of this book, I have explored and experimented with a variety of the available subliminal audio offerings in my two years of research.

Therefore, you won't have to spend the time or effort to do this yourself, or to potentially subject yourself to some dubious (or malicious) unproven audio source. You can find out more about this in the *advanced accelerator method* chapter.

The Simple, Effortless, 7-Step LENSE+GP Method

Chapter 7

The Simple, Effortless, 7-Step LENSE+GP Method

We have seen from numerous research studies that certain adaptions of Cognitive Behavioral Therapy with a mindfulness meditation, usually referred to as Mindfulness-Based Cognitive Therapy (MBCT), can provide you with *some very real and significant benefits.*

As previously referenced studies show, *you are less likely to die from a heart attack,*[1,5,15] and you have up to a *50% reduction in the likelihood of suffering a repeat bout of depression.*[11]

You are able to relax, sharpen, and focus your mind, and you are less likely to experience the pain of a destructive behavior or substance abuse, or to self-harm. You gain the ability to master your emotions, improve your memory, boost your energy levels and immune system, attain and maintain your peak performance, lower blood pressure, and alleviate tension in your muscles.[12,13,15,22,24,27,28,30]

In fact, a mindfulness meditation can positively impact almost all areas of your physical and psychological wellbeing.

As well as doing all of this, and almost as if quite by accident and incidental to the whole process, *it removes or eliminates ("banishes") your constant worry and anxiety.*

So, the challenge then was: *How could you obtain most, if not all, of these benefits, without the very considerable time and effort necessary to achieve them, and in a way that provides predictable and consistent results?*

After two years of extensive research and much experimentation, I eventually arrived at what I call my LENSE+GP method, which really is about *as effort free* as it gets, since it's based upon the combination of a particular mindfulness meditation and a specific thought control technique, combined with some scientifically proven modern technology that does most, if not all, of the work for you.

Introducing the simple, effortless, 7-step LENSE+GP method to banish your worry and anxiety – forever!

The 7 simple steps

L	Find a suitable and appropriate **Location** and environment in which to meditate.
E	Put on your **Earphones** (or headphones). Perform a quick scan of your body to establish an initial rating for your current level of tension, pain or discomfort, worry and anxiety.
N	Select your FREE Zen12 mindful mediation audio on your MP3 player and press play. Clear your mind of all thoughts and enter into the special state of **No-Mind**. Immerse yourself for 12 to 16 minutes (track level dependent).
S	When finished meditating, immediately scan your body and notice any areas of tension or discomfort, emotions or feelings, worry and anxiety you may still have and **Score** them. Compare this score against your initial rating or starting condition.
E	**Evaluate** your score to determine how much more energy and focus, less worry and anxiety, less stress, and less pain and discomfort you have relative to before your mindfulness meditation. Now go about your day more relaxed and energized.
GP	Before you retire to bed, undergo the simple 10-minute **Gratitude Process** and add 3 new items to your Gratitude List.

Repeat daily for at least 30 days.

L – Find a suitable and appropriate *Location* and environment to meditate

You already know that you can meditate at home or at work, or almost anywhere where you can do so safely, and where the environment is conducive to do so, and at almost any suitable time of the day.

It is known that the results of your meditation will be enhanced if you can make a connection with nature while you meditate, so (if at all possible) you might prefer to take a walk to your favorite place in the park or spot by the river, or to sit in the garden at home, to meditate.

Alternatively, you may prefer, like me, to meditate first thing when you awake in the morning, and then you can enjoy the benefits for the rest of your day.

Or perhaps if you are at work, you may prefer to meditate during your lunch break, or to simply find a quiet area whenever you are able to meditate.

If you are relatively new to meditation, I suggest, initially at least, that you find a *quiet or calming environment* in which to practice, free from any external stimuli that may distract or disturb you, such as a television or radio.

Make sure that any social media or other notifications you have are turned off, along with anything else that may interfere with your ability to concentrate or to focus.

If possible, choose a comfortable area to meditate, since if you are too hot or too cold you may not be able to fully concentrate or focus.

Generally, just make sure you're in a suitable and safe environment where you won't be disturbed for up to 20 minutes.

You don't need to adopt a specific position to meditate, so long as it is a comfortable position.

You can lay flat on your back, or on a comfortable bed, or just grab a comfortable chair and sit with your shoulders relaxed and place your hands comfortably and purposefully on the arms of the chair, or by your side, and adopt an upright sitting posture, but do not slouch.

If you have not selected a guided meditation track, then I suggest that you set a 20-minute timer on your MP3 player, or PC/iMac, laptop, iPhone, iPad, iPod (or whatever digital device you are using), so that you avoid the risk of unintentionally falling asleep or overrunning your allocated time.

You can also simply type *Google Timer 20 minutes* into your internet browser.

E – Put on your *Earphones* (or headphones)

Once settled in your chosen location and position, put your earphones into your ears (or headphones over them), and, once comfortable, relax and bring your focus onto your breathing.

Breathe deeply and slowly for a few breaths, holding or pausing your breath when you have fully exhaled for a count of three (or for three seconds) before continuing to breathe in. Just keep it full and very natural.

Before going any further, quickly, and without thinking, scan your body for any tension, or any discomfort or pain, or worry and anxiety, that you have at this moment.

Scan from the top of your scalp, over your forehead, down past your jaws, through your neck, down through your upper back and chest, lower back and abdomen, hips, buttocks, thighs, knees, calves, shins, ankles, feet, and toes.

Now without paying too much attention or overthinking things, rate yourself on a scale of 10 down to 1, where 10 is when you are in a highly tense and uncomfortable or painful state or completely full of worry and anxiety, and 1 is where you are deeply relaxed, with no tension or discomfort or pain or worry and anxiety.

The first time that you do this you may feel a little uncomfortable or awkward; however, don't worry as this is quite normal and rating yourself will soon become a simple and automatic thing for you to do, and it will take but a moment of your time.

As you will see shortly, this is a way of enabling you to monitor, and measure, your condition and the progress that you are making, since this is usually achieved on a gradual basis.

N – Clear your mind and enter into the special state of *No-Mind.*

Now, make sure you are comfortable, select your downloaded FREE enhanced brainwave entrainment (BWE) audio track on your MP3 player, and press play.

Note: see later paragraphs to find out all about your special enhanced brainwave entrainment meditation track, what it does, and how to use it.

Relax, close your eyes, and clear your mind.

Fully immerse yourself in the special enhanced BWE audio track, and while listening to the voice of the track's guided introduction (about four minutes), bring your focus back onto your breathing.

As before, breathe deeply and slowly for a few breaths, holding or pausing your breath when you have fully exhaled for a count of three (or for 3 seconds) before continuing to breathe in; just keep it full and very natural.

Keep your eyes closed and take two more deep, slow breaths, then continue to breathe normally and more shallowly for about one more minute.

If your mind is drawn to a part of your body that is experiencing tension, discomfort, or pain, then relax, breathe into it, then briefly tense the muscles in that part of the body. Hold that tension for 7 seconds, and then relax and let all of the tension go from your body completely.

Repeat this tension, holding and releasing for a second time before relaxing and moving on with your meditation.

Do not concern yourself if during your meditation you struggle to focus, or if your mind should wander off to other things. This is quite normal, and when you do, simply bring your attention back to your breathing and follow the rhythm of your breath.

Notice the flow of air as it fills your lungs; observe your chest as it falls, squeezing the air out of your body; notice the rise and fall of your stomach; simply observe without any judgment or further engagement.

Once you become immersed in the Zen12 meditation audio track, and as soon as you are sufficiently relaxed, seek and attain the state of *No-Mind* using the *exact process* as described in the dedicated chapter of this book (chapter 5 – "The 5 Brilliant Ways to Stop" – "Brilliant way 5: Enter the state of 'No-Mind'").

Your mind is an accumulation of impressions or thoughts, and you will come to realize that these impressions are not you. Therefore place no attachment, or engagement, or identification, or judgment on your thoughts.

Just let them remain formless and your consciousness detached from your thinking.

This detachment will lead to an incredible sense of freedom of consciousness, which you may sometimes *see* as an *image*, such as a burst of light that grows ever stronger when you are able to hold your focus on the *image*.

By keeping your focused concentration and attention on this image, you will be able to maintain the state of *No Mind* for even longer.

When seeing this image when you are in a deeply relaxed (low Alpha or Theta brainwave) state of meditation, you may also feel the image as energy pulsating through your entire body, or sometimes as a warm tingly sensation.

Notice that the intensity of this energy increases as you breathe into it, just as if you were fanning the flames of a fire.

If the image that you see appears as a burst of lavender light, you might want to focus on it: this will often appear when you are deeply relaxed, without any conscious thought and with a clear mind.

With some practice, you can concentrate your focus sufficiently to create enough energy to pulsate through your entire body, or alternatively you can focus the energy on a particular part of your body.

Lavender energy frequencies have been linked to the body's internal healing, cleansing, and purifying properties in certain cultures for decades.

They can be most helpful to you, should you have any healing, or cell regeneration, or clearing requirements.

You will find that in this pure state of *No-Mind*, you have total mental clarity and complete absence of the egoic mind, without any of your feelings of worry and anxiety.

Your mind is not empty but fully present, fully aware, and free from all of the mind's constant and repetitive noise and chatter.

You are in a state where all your questions and thoughts dissolve and evaporate. Your egoic mind withdraws, leaving you in a state of pure existence, with only your breathing, the image of your energy, and the feeling of your pulsating heart.

You are completely immersed in the present moment, with no past or imagined future, and *no worry or anxiety*… enjoy!

Please note, your FREE Zen12 meditation audio track is highly recommended for the quickest results with the least amount of effort. Just go to the web address in the Introduction or the Resources chapter of this book.

However, if you are not accustomed to meditation and don't wish to download your FREE audio track, then I suggest you consider experimenting with the specially created, and adapted, progressive muscle relaxation based meditation provided for you in the Appendix.

Alternatively, if you have acquired the full Zen12 program and are at a more advanced stage, at level 7 or 12 (the very best level for its amazing benefits), you will most likely want to skip the first spoken introduction part of the Zen12 guided track (some four minutes or so) and transition straight into the meditation, and into the state of *No-Mind*.

After a few attempts of doing this, you will find that you can achieve this very easily and naturally, and with less and less effort, while still being able to remove all thoughts from your mind (*and thus all worry and anxiety*). You will then be able to enjoy approximately four minutes more of mediation (at a very deep level).

When your meditation session has finished, you will be in a serene and relaxed state, which will continue to exist for some time afterward, and your mind will continue to work at its most optimum, providing you with enhanced focus, creativity, and productivity.

S – *Scan* your body for tension or discomfort, emotions or feelings, and *Score* or grade them

Immediately after your meditation, scan your body again (just as before) for any remaining tension, pain, discomfort, worry, or anxiety, and 'Score' them using the same previous rating system, where 10 is you being in a highly tense and uncomfortable or painful state or completely full of worry and anxiety, and 1 is where you are deeply relaxed with no tension or discomfort or pain, or worry and anxiety.

Now compare this new rated score against the previous score at the start of your meditation.

E – *Evaluate* how much more energy, less worry and anxiety, and less pain and discomfort you have

Evaluate your rating *'Scores'* in terms of:

a. the reduction in the level of your worry and anxiety

b. your progress, or general improvement, in terms of how much more energy, and how much less general stress, pain or discomfort, that you now have... compared to when you *first used* the LENSE method

c. how long this new rating, and its associated state of mind and general improvement, lasts as you go about your (normal) daily tasks and routine.

Repeat these simple steps of the LENSE method on a consistent daily basis (which should take you no more than 20 minutes) for a minimum of 30 consecutive days, since that is the time most researchers suggest is a minimum needed to create a new habit and to change your results.

Historically, Dr. Maxwell Maltz suggested it took 21 days to change a habit; however, the average time is now thought to be 66 days, or more specifically 21 to 254 days. I found 30 days was typical for the LENSE method.

This is the time it takes for your brain to *"rewire itself,"* or *establish a new dominant neurological pathway.*[41,42]

Consistent daily practice of the LENSE method creates the necessary reframing and repositioning of your beliefs, your understanding, and your experiences.

These will then change your thinking, and your thoughts will change your feelings and emotions, and therefore your results or outcomes.

With consistency it becomes ever easier for you to achieve the desired outcome, and the effects last for much longer.

You will then only need to don your headphones, relax, hit the play button on your MP3 player, and simply listen during your scheduled daily 20-minute time slot.

So just imagine, if you dare, how it would feel after 30 days to finally experience the sheer bliss of being free of all your worry and anxiety.

To be free from all the constant mind noise and chatter, free of all of those "*what if*" fear-based thoughts.

To finally have a clear and focused mind that is ready to serve you – image how that feels!

GP – A simple, 10-minute *Gratitude Process* (before bedtime)

Having successfully achieved a newfound state of mind that was free from worry and anxiety by using the LENSE method (in the early morning), something that I wrestled with for many months was how to consistently maintain this blissful state throughout the entire day.

What typically happens is that you achieve the newfound state of mind, and it lasts for a short period of time, and then you gradually revert back to your previous state of constant worry and anxiety.

The period of time usually depends upon the challenges that your day holds for you, for example the number and types of meetings you have, or the types of people that you meet or work with.

But first, I need to be quite clear about something. If you were to ask me if this newly found worry and anxiety free state of mind had somehow magically been achieved, after only a 20-minute combined mindful meditation and *No-Mind* session, and that was it, 'job done' forever, I would of course have to say to you... *Don't be so ridiculous.*

After all, I have lived with this inherited and environmentally conditioned state of mind (my constant worry and anxiety) for decades.

It would simply be totally unrealistic to think it would just somehow *disappear* overnight, never to return.

In any case, your clever egoic mind would almost certainly make sure this didn't happen, since (as we have already learned) part of its very existence depends on keeping you in your fear-based worry and anxiety state of mind.

To find a way, then, to basically allow me to enjoy this newfound state of mind all day long, and to do this in a way that involves the least amount of effort, meant that something else was needed to support, reinforce, and supplement the LENSE method.

After much experimentation, trial, and error, I found that the best and most effective way of achieving this reinforcement and supplementation was, surprisingly, to apply a simple *Gratitude Process.*

Yes, a simple *Gratitude Process* where you first create a Gratitude List, and then you:

a. read through and reflect (on each item) of your Gratitude List, for about five minutes

b. then spend five minutes more thinking about your day, find the three most significant things that you are truly grateful for, then add these to your list at the end of each day, before retiring to bed.

In a large study in the *Journal of Personality and Social Psychology* by the American Psychological Association, psychologists from the Universities of California and Miami carried out experiments to determine what effects a *grateful outlook* had on the psychological and physical wellbeing of a number of different groups of people.[49]

They found that the group with a *gratitude outlook* exhibited heightened wellbeing outcomes, with emotional and interpersonal (amongst other) benefits.

Research from other studies have also shown that keeping a Gratitude List (or 'Blessings Log') can make you happier, reduce your stress and *your worry.*[50,51]

However, the process by which you accomplish this is critical to its success.

Very often, people fail to achieve the expected outcome when it is not done in a very particular way.

It is critically important that you have a genuine gratitude for the something, or someone, that you add to your Gratitude List.

You need to feel connected to people, and to make a habit to thank them for being in your life and to truly appreciate them for what they have done, or for the insights they have provided, their teaching or coaching, or for whatever it is that they may have given or done for you.

You must be truly and genuinely grateful for whatever they have achieved, for who they are and whatever they have meant to you or done for you. This is critical to the success of the whole Gratitude Process.

The Gratitude Process

This starts with you creating for yourself a Gratitude List, a list of at least 10 things that you are genuinely most grateful for.

When you have created your list, then at the end of each day before retiring to bed, you spend about five minutes just briefly reflecting on each item on your Gratitude List as you scan through it.

Then, without overthinking things, you spend another five minutes or so thinking about your day and finding the three most significant things that you are truly grateful for, and then you simply add these things to your Gratitude List.

This process will inevitably become quicker as you become more accustomed to the simple process, and the increased speed in which you are able to scan and reflect on the items on your list will naturally compensate for the expanding number of items on your list, at least in the short term.

On a longer-term basis, you can rotate the items or simply focus on the last page.

To help you to get started with your own Gratitude List, I have provided below some items you might typically expect to find on the list, just to help stimulate your thinking.

However, remember *your* Gratitude List needs to reflect items that *you* are truly and genuinely grateful for.

Start your Gratitude List by writing as a title or heading the words (as often said by the great Bob Proctor of the Proctor and Gallagher Institute): "*I am so happy and grateful (now) that I have…*" in bold or underlined writing, and then make a list of at least 10 things that you are truly and sincerely grateful for.

For example, "*I am so happy and grateful (now) that I have…*"

a. overcome a particular health or welfare challenge or issue
b. the support of a partner, or a particular friend, parent, or child, or a cousin or neighbor, or a work colleague
c. a new home, or one that has been specifically adapted to meet your needs or requirements; friendly neighbors, or a favorite local shop or café
d. the opportunity to see, or spend time with, your children or grandchildren
e. a sense of fulfillment from providing a service or support to a close friend, or relative, or charity
f. easy access to a favorite walk in the countryside, park, wood, or beach, or by a river or lake
g. a time-saving kitchen gadget
h. a particular model of car or transport vehicle (SUV, open-top sports car, Tesla, etc.)
i. achieved a wealth goal or milestone (paying off your mortgage or student loan) or reached financial independence
j. a special friendship or relationship
k. the means to afford regular or exciting meals out, or holidays abroad, or just to escape the cold of winter or the heat of summer
l. the good fortune to be part of an ethical business or profession
m. the chance to be an inspirational mentor to a friend or family member, or a business or work colleague

n. the opportunity to provide coaching or teaching on something you love or deeply care about

o. skill or aptitude at a particular sport, hobby, or activity (playing the drums, guitar, running, football, swimming, fishing, shooting, etc.)

Once you get started with creating your list, you will probably be surprised just how quickly you begin to recall different aspects, situations, or circumstances that really matter to you and that you are genuinely grateful for.

Don't worry if some of the things on your Gratitude List appear at first to be relatively minor when compared to the worldwide news and global events of the day – what matters is that they have significance, relevance, and meaning to you.

For example, it could just be getting to somewhere, or meeting someone that is important to you, sharing a coffee with a friend or colleague, something nice that someone has said to you, a smile or just getting out of bed and feeling energized, or finishing a report, or a safe journey.

Alternatively, it could be something really major like getting the all-clear from your cancer treatment!

Remember sometimes we don't fully appreciate aspects of our life situation or circumstances, or our experiences, until we can no longer engage or participate in them: for example, being able to play a favorite sport, or going for a walk in the park or countryside, or to a beach, or simply playing with or looking after a child or grandchild.

It really does not matter how relatively big or small the items you add to your list are, so long as they are genuinely meaningful to you.

As we have already learned, something happens when you place your attention and focus on what you are genuinely grateful for, and this results in you receiving (eventually) more of the same or similar things or experiences.

By writing these items down and adding them to your Gratitude List, you create within you a deeper appreciation and emotional connection to them, and you will think less about what you *wish for* (your *"if only"* and *"what if"* fear-based thoughts).

You might also recall from previous chapters that you need to just *accept* the things and situations and circumstances that you find yourself in (and that you don't want in your life) for being *"what they are."*

In other words, acknowledge and accept your circumstances or situation *"as it is,"* without any judgment or further reflection or engagement on your part of any kind.

When you adopt this simple Gratitude Process, in this exact and particular way, this creates within you a frame of mind based upon an understanding and appreciation of *what you have* rather than *what you don't have*, or *what you wish you had*.

Finally, take note that whatever thoughts your mind focuses on, you will (eventually) receive more of (delayed gratification). However, you need to be very careful with this – not just because it is so powerful (and it is) – but look *very carefully* at the detail.

For example, if your thoughts are saying, *I wish that I could worry less and be less anxious*, this will of course deliver to you exactly that… *more wishing you were able to worry less and more wishing you were less anxious*.

Whereas saying, *I am so happy and grateful now that I am completely free of all worry and anxiety and feel so calm and relaxed*, will (eventually) *provide you with less worry and less anxiety, with a greater feeling of being calm and relaxed*.

I am sure you get the idea! But, as always, make sure you pay particular attention to the details.

What is special about the Zen12 program, and how do I use it?

During my research, I explored and experimented with a variety of brainwave entrainment (BWE) audio offerings.

This means that you don't have to spend the time, or effort, to do so, or to incur the cost of doing so.

Perhaps even more importantly, you don't have to subject yourself to the potential harm or damage from some potentially dubious or malicious supplier – this is, after all, being played directly to your subconscious brain.

Unfortunately, not all BWE programs are of the same quality, or meet the same standards, so for your own safety it is very important that you are certain of what exactly your subconscious brain is being exposed to.

As the audio tracks are specially enhanced with advanced BWE frequencies and techniques, it is suggested by the producer that you only listen to them once a day, and do not listen to them while driving or in charge of or operating machinery, or if you suffer from epilepsy (always check the product safety instructions before use and consult your physician).

Figure 3: Zen12, reprinted by courtesy of Inspire3 Ltd, London, UK[53]

The BWE audio program that I have found works the best for me, and is particularly effective at addressing worry and anxiety – the program I use every day – is the Zen12 meditation program, which comes from the well-established and reputable UK-based company Inspire3 Ltd.[53]

The Zen12 program has specific encoded frequencies, or isochronic tones, that are blended with other entrainment techniques that take you down very quickly into a very deep state of meditation.

As the audio sounds influence your brainwaves, they naturally quieten your mind and relax your body, reducing all of your mental noise and chatter, melting away your stress, your worry, and your anxiety.

It does all of this effortlessly, and as you go into a deeper state of meditation it triggers the release of the chemical serotonin, which is well known to boost your mood or *happiness* level.

This technology is particularly helpful in overcoming the typical problems associated with meditation, such as not having the time, or confidence, necessary to successfully and consistently meditate, or not being able to fully concentrate or focus, or finding that you cannot quieten your mind, or you become easily distracted, or you find meditation boring, or just too time consuming.

Zen12 has 12 distinct levels, from 1 to 12. With each higher level the BWE frequencies get lower and lower, helping you to access deeper and deeper states of meditation.

You reach the deeper state faster with each level, bringing with it therefore more benefits and better results with every new higher level.

Each level is designed in such a way for you to listen daily for around a month, before you move on to the next level.

However, if you are experienced in meditation you might typically start at level 7 and see what results you achieve.

If you are not getting the full benefit at that level, then simply drop back to a lower level, say level 5, and see how you manage with this for a week. Then advance to the next level if you feel you are ready to do so, or select the next level down if you have any uncertainties.

Your FREE downloadable meditation track with enhanced BWE is a level 1 audio track and lasts for 12 minutes.

It takes you gently down from your natural Beta brainwave (starting) state down to a 10 Hz Alpha brainwave frequency, which is associated with mood elevation, serotonin release, and pain control.

As the session ends, it brings you back to a low Beta frequency, leaving you feeling relaxed, refreshed, and alert for the rest of your day.

I think you will agree, it's a great starting point for your meditation adventure and a sound basis for you to build from.

The overall time for each of the BWE audio tracks, from level 1 through to and including level 7, is 12 minutes.

The track time then gradually increases for higher levels to a total of 20 minutes for level 12.

If you should decide to progress and invest in the full Zen12 program, then you are in for a real treat, as Level 12 takes you gently down to a Theta brainwave state of 7 Hz.

115

This is the same frequency measured by experienced Zen monks who have typically practiced mediation for four to six hours a day and for many decades (22 years of daily practice equates to around 40,000 hours of meditation).

At the end of the Zen12 audio track, you are gently brought back to the usual Beta brainwave frequency state.

The 20 minutes of meditation has been shown to be equivalent to over an hour's deep "Zen monk" level of meditation.

Figure 4: Zen12. Reprinted by courtesy of Inspire3 Ltd, London, UK[53]

This represents a huge saving in time and effort, without you having to face the many challenges of meditation, such as committing to the many hours of practice (~40,000 hours) that is required to successfully achieve the advanced level of meditation necessary when using a traditional method of meditation (on a consistent and predictable basis).

A research study using MRI scanners showed that even a 20-minute-a-day meditation for four days reduced anxiety levels by 39%.[40]

Another study showed that a similar 20-minute daily session of meditation, for five days, resulted in increased attention, self-regulation, and vigor, and a reduction in cortisol, anxiety, anger, and fatigue.[28]

While you don't have to listen every day, I strongly recommend that you do so to achieve the quickest possible results.

Simply schedule Zen12 into your busy daily life.

I found the benefits of using the Zen12 program are more predictable and consistent than any other of the meditation options I researched and used, and the benefits are almost instant.

Very soon my usual worry and anxiety just melted away, and it leaves you feeling more relaxed, calmer, and happier.

For every level in the Zen12 program, there are four different types of audio mixes, or *flavors,* for you to choose from, depending on the mood and circumstances or situation that you are in at the time.

These flavors are the *Relaxation Mix* (a soothing spa-like background music), the *Sounds of Nature* (countryside sounds and babbling brooks), the *White Noise* (a sort of fuzzy sound that blocks out background distractions), and finally a guided meditation mix.

The guided meditation mix has a brief spoken introduction only at the very start of the track, has a relaxing audio backdrop, then ends the track with a spoken 5 to 1 countdown.

The guided meditation mix has the advantage that you won't have to set a timer to ensure you don't overrun your session, which is very helpful when you are on a very tight or busy work, or life, schedule.

You just listen to the *flavor* you prefer, or that suits your circumstances or your situation at that particular moment, or just simply do what I almost always do and use the guided meditation option, or *flavor*, since this sets the scene and manages your session's start and completion.

When you are experienced with the Zen12 meditation (after the first 30 days or so), you can most likely skip the first ~4 minutes of the guided meditation track.

At this more advanced stage, you probably do not need to follow the mediation process exactly as previously described in the LENSE method but can go straight into the state of *No-Mind*.

When your meditation session has finished, you will be in a serene, calm, and relaxed state, which will continue to exist for some time afterward.

Your mind continues to work at its most optimum, providing you with enhanced focus, creativity, and productivity.

For me, it simply doesn't get any simpler or easier than this – to experience a full one hour's worth of deep meditation, all in 12 minutes, with a proven level of ease and consistency.

All you have to do is hit your play button on your MP3 player and discover for yourself the power of the unique Zen12 program with its advanced brainwave entrainment frequencies.

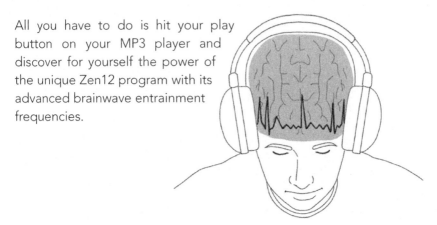

Are there any alternative programs to Zen12?

Good question. Yes, other programs do exist and are available!

However, they tend to be incredibly expensive, often use older and out-of-date or less effective and efficient BWE technologies, and many have unnecessary and expensive extra elements that I found you do not actually need.

There is a more advanced, and more expensive, BWE program from the same provider as Zen12 called the *"Brain Evolution System"* (BES).[44] It is also as quick and simple to use, and although it offers greater flexibility it takes 30 minutes a day (rather than 12 to 20 minutes).

I suggest you might consider the BES as an upgrade to the Zen12 program, and unless you are determined only to have the very best from the outset, *regardless of cost*, I suggest you might in the first instance at least try the Zen12 program, which is what I use every day.

Your FREE Zen12 (level 1) 12-minute track can be easily claimed by you: just visit the direct web address provided in the resource chapter of this book, also given below:

https://www.zen12.com/gift/a/thebestyou

For completeness I have also provided a link to the BES program in the resource chapter of this book should you want any further details.

The Optional Advanced Accelerator Technique

Chapter 8

The Optional Advanced Accelerator Technique

If you wish to do, so you can accelerate your progress toward achieving a newfound worry and anxiety free state of mind, and maintaining it, even more easily, using what I call the Optional Advanced Accelerator Technique (OAAT).

Although I was able to acquire and maintain my worry and anxiety free state of mind for the entire day when using a combination of the LENSE method (in the early morning) and the Gratitude Process (last thing in the day before retiring to bed), for me this took a relatively long period of time (over three months).

This was achieved by the consistent daily use of the LENSE+GP method, and of course the end result was very much worth it, in terms of all of the benefits that I was then able to enjoy.

This was particularly so as the LENSE+GP method would only take me less than 30 minutes a day in total to maintain it.

However, looking back on the whole process, or the journey, over those months of ups and downs and frustration, I felt there must be a better and quicker way to achieve and maintain the benefits throughout the day.

Then, quite out of the blue and almost by accident, I was offered a free trial of any of the *Subliminal Guru* audios from those nice folks at Inspire3 (they are generous like that – or at least occasionally...), so guess which track I picked from their catalogue? Yes, you're right – I picked the *Stop Worrying* audio track.

I was so impressed with the results I achieved from using this audio track that I reviewed their entire catalogue and began experimenting with various offerings and options.

From this research and experimentation, of the various options in their catalogue (at that time), I found two particular and complementary products, one audio and one visual, that led me to discover what I now call the OAAT.

I found the best products to accelerate the transition to a worry and anxiety free state of mind were two complementary but separate types of subliminals that, when used together, enhanced and reinforced the LENSE+GP method.

This combination is the *Subliminal Guru* audio track, *Stop Worrying* with brainwave entrainment (BWE), and the *Subliminal 360* software, the science of which (BWE and subliminals) we have already reviewed and evaluated in an earlier chapter.[52,54]

The *Subliminal Guru albums* have different subliminal messages embed within them to cover a number of different targeted subjects (fears, phobias, worry, etc.).

reprinted by courtesy of Inspire3 Ltd, London, UK[52]

Subliminal Guru albums can be used almost anywhere and at any time, to speed up and *boost* your rapid progress toward the elimination, or reduction, of your worry and anxiety.

There are seven variations or mixes for each of the Subliminal Guru audio tracks, to match the mood or situation you are in or you wish to create.

I usually select the *Relaxation* or *Acoustic* soundtrack, or mix, unless I need more motivation, or when I am in the gym, or on a brisk walk, when I will select and play the higher tempo *Workout* track mix.

I occasionally will listen to the *Spoken Subliminals with Brainwaves* mix, as this *talks* to your conscious mind and you can clearly hear all of the subliminal messages that are used in all of the track mixes.

Although I have no scientific evidence to support this, listening to the subliminal messages appears to lower your resistance (from your egoic mind) to accepting the (positive) changes.

It also answers the basic question of *what exactly are the subliminal messages that I am subjecting my unconscious mind to?* and removes any concerns you may have as to the actual message content.

You can listen to the ten-minute audio tracks as frequently as you wish, although of course I would never listen to anything while driving, or in charge of or operating machinery.

I listen all the time while I am in the office, or out walking, going to the shops, or using public transport, or in the gym, or walking in the park or to the shops.

I simply put my earphones into my ears from my music player (my iPhone, iPad, iPod, or if sitting at my desk my iMac or laptop) and listen to one or more of my chosen mixes, or simply leave one on as a continuous loop.

You need to listen to the audio track for a minimum of 30 consecutive days, since that is the time most researchers suggest is the minimum needed to create a new habit and to change your results, or the time it takes for your brain to *"rewire itself"* (establish a new dominant neurological pathway).[42]

Historically, Dr. Maxwell Maltz thought it took 21 days to change a habit. However, the latest research suggests this can vary from 21 to 254 days, with the average time thought to be 66 days. I found it to be around 30 days for the *Subliminal Guru* tracks, dependent upon the frequency of use.

Subliminal 360

This is an easy and fun to use piece of software that works by flashing selected positive affirmations (or ones that you have created yourself) visually onto your computer screen, or digital device, for just a few milliseconds at a time.

The software comes complete with a number of pre-loaded and ready-to-use lists of affirmations, from which you can simply select the entire list, or modify, change, or delete any entry in the list.

Alternatively, you can manually create and select your own list of applicable bespoke affirmations.

You can easily adjust the frequency and display time of the selected affirmations, which momentarily flash on your screen, to match your own preferences or your visual sensitivities, and these are then displayed on your screen in randomly allocated positions or locations.

You can review your affirmations at any time and edit them in any way you wish, or further modify them as you see fit.

However, you should always look *very carefully* at the detail of each affirmation, in the same way as we did when reviewing our expressions of gratitude on our Gratitude List in a previous chapter.

You need to avoid affirmations that might say something such as *I wish to reduce and eliminate all of my worry and anxiety,* as this will of course deliver you *more wishing you were able to reduce and eliminate all of your worry and anxiety.*

Whereas saying *I am so happy and grateful now that I am completely free of all worry and anxiety and feel so calm and relaxed,* will of course *provide you with less worry and less anxiety,* eventually (the law of delayed gratification).

The Subliminal 360 software therefore provides you with complete control over what you see and how long you see it for!

The overall effect is one that does not distract your focus in any way from whatever you are doing on your PC/Mac or laptop.

As explained in the chapter on subliminals, your subconscious mind observes, stores, and processes these momentarily displayed affirmations in a way that is almost invisible to your conscious mind and its associated filters and controls, thereby effectively bypassing your conscious mind.

The constant background repetition of the affirmations helps the messaging within the affirmations to become deeply embedded within your subconscious mind, displacing and overwriting reframing your existing learned or inherited beliefs and habits.[42]

Therefore, they will help you change how you think, and therefore your feelings and emotions, and therefore your actions and your results.

Or as Dr. Joseph Murphy writes in his book *The Power of Your Subconscious Mind*; "change your thoughts, and you change your destiny."[43]

Like most technologies, nothing is for everyone, and it is essential when reviewing your affirmations that you also take note of any health or safety warning notices provided with any subliminal products. Also note that suffers of epilepsy are generally advised not use such products.

Please also note that not all brainwave entrainment or subliminal audio or visual programs (or products) are the same. They can vary considerably in terms of quality and therefore potential risks.

With these products from Inspire3, you can clearly see and review the subliminal messages you are using, which is so important since you should always be certain of what exactly you are exposing your subconscious brain to.

Personally, I would only use products that come from a known, recognized, and reputable sound engineering laboratory or audio studio.

You should of course always do your own suitable and sufficient risk assessment, your own due diligence, and consult with your physician or healthcare advisor prior to the use of such products.

I continue to use this combination almost every single day, and have done so for over a year, and I have found that, for me at least, the OAAT not only speeds up your progress but also helps you to avoid slipping back into your previous worry and anxiety state of mind.

A kind of insurance policy then, if you wish.

Appendix: Beginner's Guide to Meditation

Beginner's Guide to Meditation

As we have seen in earlier chapters of this book, a mindfulness meditation can provide you with some amazing *physical, emotional, cogitative, and behavioral benefits*. In fact mindfulness meditation seems to have something to offer almost everyone.

As the referenced studies show, you are *less likely to die from a heart attack,*[1,5,15] and you have up to *a 50% reduction in suffering a repeat bout of depression.*[11]

You are less likely to experience the pain of a destructive behavior, or substance abuse, or to self-harm. It will improve digestive disorders, help you to master your emotions, relax, sharpen and focus your mind, improve your memory, boost your energy levels and immune system, attain and maintain your peak performance, lower your blood pressure, and alleviate tension in your muscles.[12,13,15,22,24,27,28,30]

In fact, it seems that a mindfulness meditation can positively impact almost all areas of your physical and psychological wellbeing.

The LENSE+GP method makes use of the special brainwave-enhanced Zen12 meditation audio track. At level 12 this is a 20-minute meditation that offers you the potential to enjoy up to 15 minutes in the special state of "No-Mind," and from it a proven thought control technique.

You can download your very own FREE copy of the highly specialized brainwave-enhanced Zen12 guided meditation track from our website simply by visiting the website direct at this address:

https://www.zen12.com/gift/a/thebestyou

You can then just put on your headphones (or earphones), get yourself comfortable in your preferred location and position, press play, and drift into a deeply relaxing meditation.

Why not let modern technology help you in a way that has never before been available – and get all of the benefits that only a mindfulness meditation can give you?

Please note, your FREE Zen12 meditation audio track is highly recommended for the quickest results with the least amount of effort from the LENSE+GP method – just click on the link above.

What is unique about this meditation?

However, if for whatever reason you do not wish to download your FREE specially enhanced meditation track, and you are new to meditation, then the following adapted Progressive Muscle Relaxation (PMR) based meditation below has been developed for you.

You are probably aware that there are several different ways, or *styles*, in which to meditate, including those that use a *mantra* or *chanting* (quietly to yourself or aloud), a focused meditation (usually with an image or a particular object or smell), and mindfulness meditation, to name just some of the most popular *styles*.

One of the simplest ways to practice a traditional style of meditation is to focus on the breath, as the breath and mind work in tandem: as your breath begins to lengthen, your brainwaves begin to slow down.

The meditation provided below adapts one such form of traditional meditation, with a *shortened version* of the PMR technique, developed from the work of Dr. Edmund Jacobson in the 1930s as a useful aid to *reduce patients' anxiety levels*, to help them overcome their fatigue issues and be able to think more rationally.

It incorporates a classical countdown relaxation meditation, which should be helpful to create the right physical and mental environment for you to enter into the deep level of meditation that is necessary, should you wish to do so, to enter into the special state of *No-Mind* and enjoy the many benefits of this thought control technique.

In order to become very relaxed, you will need to tense up and then relax groups of opposing sets of muscles.

You proceed through a series of these movements, and the cumulative effects of relaxation will then be felt over your entire body.

You will need to tense each group of your muscles for about 7 seconds, then immediately release them, and then focus on the relaxed muscles for a further 15 seconds, before moving onto another muscle group. This increases the level of relaxation more than just letting go of the tension.

Do not worry about, or pay particular attention to, any tingling or warmth or heaviness sensations or feelings you may experience, as this is normal.

The intention here is to tighten and tense your muscles, not to strain them or create any pain or injury.

Preparation for your meditation

To begin your first meditation, *find a quiet or calming environment* in which to practice, free from any external stimuli that may distract or disturb you, such as the television or radio.

Ensure that any social media notifications are turned off, along with anything else that may interfere with your ability to concentrate or focus.

If possible, choose a comfortable area to meditate, since if you are too cold or too hot you may not be able to fully concentrate or focus.

Generally, make sure you're in a suitable and safe place or area where you won't be disturbed.

Do not concern yourself if, during your meditation, you struggle to focus, or if your mind should wander off to other things – this is normal. When this happens, simply bring your attention back to your breathing and follow the rhythm of your breath.

According to Professor Øyvind Ellingsen of the Norwegian University of Science and Technology, a very experienced practitioner of meditation:

> *Spontaneous wandering of the mind is something you become more aware of and familiar with when you meditate.*

This default activity of the brain is often underestimated. It probably represents a kind of mental processing that connects various experiences and emotional residues, puts them into perspective and lays them to rest.

When you get up at the end of your meditation session, do so slowly and stretch out like a cat stretches after sleeping, to avoid you losing your state of relaxation, or you feeling slightly dizzy (due to changes in your blood pressure).

You can meditate by either lying flat on your back or on a comfortable bed, or sitting in a comfortable chair. Always provide any additional support necessary for your head or neck if needed.

Let's assume you have a comfortable location and position in which to sit for twenty minutes and you prefer to sit in a comfortable chair.

Now, with your shoulders relaxed and spine upright, place your legs comfortably at right angles to the floor and uncrossed, and place your arms by your sides.

I suggest you set a 20-minute timer on your MP3 player, or on your PC/Mac, laptop, iPhone, iPad, iPod, or watch, so that you avoid the risk of unintentionally falling asleep or overrunning your allocated time.

(Tip: you can type *Google timer 20 mins* into any browser.)

Now you are ready – let us start the meditation together

Close your eyes and make yourself as comfortable as you can. Settle back comfortably into your chair. Now take a full deep breath: breathe right in and hold it for a count of three (or three seconds)… and now exhale. Just try to let go of all the tension in your body.

Let the air out quite automatically. Notice a calmer feeling beginning to develop.

Carry on breathing normally and just concentrate on feeling heavy all over in a pleasant way. Study your own body heaviness. This should give you a calm and reassuring feeling all over.

As you continue to breathe, simply notice the flow of air as it fills your lungs, and observe your chest as it falls, squeezing the air out of your body. Notice the rise and fall of your stomach. Simply observe without any judgment or further engagement.

Now concentrate on your hands and your arms and forget about the rest of your body.

Make as tight a fist as you can with both hands. Tense the muscles of your lower forearms and press your elbows into the back of the chair. Now bend both of your elbows and slowly and fully tense your bicep muscles. Hold the tension for the count of 7 (or 7 seconds) and note the sensation of tension in the muscles. And relax…(immediately release the tension).

Study the difference between the tension and relaxation of the muscles. Notice that relaxing is an active movement. Notice how the muscles feel as they become more relaxed.

Just try to let these muscles relax further and further. There is nothing else you have to be concerned about at this time except relaxing.

Once more, with both of your hands, clench your fists and press your elbows into the back of the chair. Now bend both of your elbows and slowly and fully tense your bicep muscles. Hold the tension… *and relax*!

Let your arms drop down by your sides and straighten your fingers; feel the tension draining away. Just let go and unwind, letting the muscles relax further and further.

As you tense and relax various muscle groups, you might feel a tingling sensation as the relaxation flows in, or you might have a warm sensation. Whatever you feel, I want you to notice it and enjoy it to the full, as the relaxation spreads further and further.

Now turn your attention to the muscles in your head region.

Squint your eyes together tightly, clench your jaws together, push your teeth together, pull the sides of your mouth outward, concentrate on the tension in your facial muscles, and hold it… *and relax…* relax your jaws now, relax your eyes, relax your mouth, let your lips part slightly, and let your eyelids rest.

Appreciate the relaxation as it spreads all over your face, your forehead, your scalp, and your eyes and jaws – there's nothing else to be concerned about now except relaxing.

Now concentrate on your neck muscles. Press your head back as far as it will go. Feel the tension in your neck, monitor the feeling of tautness there… and hold the tension… *and relax.* Let the tension go completely, and notice the feeling of relief from tensing and relaxing your muscles. Carry on breathing normally.

Now turn your attention to the muscles in the shoulders, chest, and stomach.

Take a slow, deep breath, throw your chest out, bring your shoulder blades together, and pull on the muscles of the stomach. Concentrate on the tension; hold it… *and relax…* let your shoulders drop and your stomach muscles relax, and carry on breathing normally and easily.

Let your breathing return to its normal regular pattern.

Concentrate on the difference in sensation between tension and relaxation, and continue breathing normally and easily. Let the tension dissolve as the relaxation grows deeper and deeper.

Each time you breathe out, notice the rhythmic relaxation in your lungs and in your stomach.

Now focus your attention on the muscles of your thighs, calves, and feet. Concentrate on your legs and forget about the rest of your body.

Press your heals down into the floor while curling the toes downward. Curl the toes away from you, notice the feelings of tension in your thighs and in your shins, and study the tension… hold the tension… *and relax.*

Keep relaxing and monitor the feeling. Notice the warm feeling of relaxation and continue to breathe normally.

Let yourself relax further and further. Relax all areas of your body and feel the heaviness of your body as you relax even further; just let go as you become more and more relaxed.

Now explore your body from the feet up. Make sure that every muscle is relaxed: first your toes, then your feet, your legs, buttocks, stomach, shoulders, neck, eyes, and finally your forehead – all should be relaxed now.

Each time you practice this routine you should find a deeper level of relaxation being achieved, a deep, calm feeling.

To increase the feelings of relaxation further as you exhale, each time you breathe out, for the next one minute I want you to think of the word "relax" to yourself. Just think the word *relax* as you breathe out. Now do that for the next one minute.

Feel the heavy sensations that accompany relaxation as your muscles switch off and you feel calm and secure, and as you breathe out you feel all the tension leaving you.

Now visualize in your mind's eye that you are standing at the top of a large, winding staircase with ten steps. It is your private staircase and you know it well; you feel very comfortable being there.

This staircase leads you down into what you consider to be a very *special place*, a place you know well and where you feel comfortable: perhaps a garden paradise, or a tranquil green valley, or even a tropical island beach with white sand, clear blue water, and an amazing view – whatever you consider to be your special place.

It is a place you consider to be your most perfect vision of paradise.

In a moment, I will ask you to count down from 10 to 1. Every time you count down a number, you take another step slowly down the staircase, to your *special place*, and as you do so you go deeper and deeper into a state of relaxation.

When you reach the count of 1, imagine you have reached the bottom of the staircase; you will then find yourself in your most perfect vision of paradise, a place of perfect peace and calm.

Now imagine yourself walking slowly down the staircase, and as you move down each step, you relax deeper and deeper. With each count you will relax more and more as you go deeper and deeper into a state of profound relaxation.

The countdown

Start to count: 10 – and you take your first step; 9 – relaxing more and more deeply; 8 – a deeper and deeper relaxation; 7 – gently walking down the stairs; 6 – you feel more and more relaxed; 5 – going deeper and deeper; 4 – you are serene and calm; 3 – you are very relaxed; 2 – going ever deeper and deeper; 1 – very, very, profoundly relaxed as you gently step off the bottom step and into a perfectly relaxed and calm place of perfect peace.

Imagine yourself now lying on a beach on a warm summer day, and notice the sensations you feel as you lie in the sun. The sun is a very bright golden yellow, the sky a brilliant blue, and the sand a dazzling white that glistens in the sunlight.

Notice the breeze as it blows over you, how it feels in contrast to the heat of the sun. Taste and smell the salt in the air, and hear the rhythm of the breaking waves, a rhythmic flapping to and fro, back and forth, of the water against the shore.

You can hear the far-off cry of a distant gull. Notice the warmth of the sun on your face!

There is nothing else for you to be concerned about except to relax, to be calm and tranquil, more and more comfortable, tranquil, serene, relaxed, breathing slowly and gently, thoughts slowing down, time slowing down, lots of time, so much time.

Your mind and body are slowing down, arms relaxing, legs relaxing, face relaxing, body and mind relaxing, warm and comfortable, at peace, calm, more and more relaxed and drowsy, becoming more and more deeply relaxed, peaceful, quiet, drifting, floating, as your relaxation goes deeper and deeper.

Now stay like this for about one more minute, and then I want you to count backward from 5 to I, and when you reach the number 1, I want you to open your eyes and you will feel very calm and refreshed, pleasantly warm and relaxed.

5 – becoming aware of your breathing; 4 – beginning to feel more alert; 3 – getting ready to start stretching and moving; 2 – fully aware of your

surroundings; 1 – eyes wide open, fully awake, feeling very relaxed, warm, calm, and alert.

Congratulations you have completed your meditation

When your meditation session has finished, your serene and relaxed state will continue to exist for some time afterward, and your mind continue to work at its most optimum, providing you with enhanced focus, creativity, and productivity.

Your mind is an accumulation of impressions or thoughts, and you will come to realize that these impressions are not you.

Therefore, place no attachment or engagement or identification or judgment on your thoughts, just let them remain formless and your consciousness detached from your thinking.

This leads to an incredible sense of freedom of consciousness, which at certain times during your meditation you may see as an image, such as a burst of light, that grows ever stronger when you are able to hold and focus on this image.

You will often feel this image while in a deeply relaxed state as energy pulsating through your entire body (or sometimes as a warm tingly sensation); notice that its intensity increases as you breathe into and out of it, just as if you were fanning the flames of a fire.

Want to enhance your meditation even further?

This is the perfect time for you to enter into the state of mind referred to as "No-Mind," exactly as detailed in an earlier chapter of this book.

In this pure state of No-Mind, you have total mental clarity and complete absence of the egoic mind You are without any of your worry and anxiety; your mind is not empty but fully present, fully aware, and free from all of your mind's constant and repetitive noise and chatter.

You are in a state where all your questions and thoughts dissolve and evaporate. Your egoic mind withdraws, leaving you in a state of pure existence, with only your breathing and the image of your energy and the feeling of your pulsating heart.

You have become completely immersed with the present moment with no past or imagined future and *no worry or anxiety*... enjoy!

Disclaimers

General disclaimer

This book is based upon the *author's real life experiences*. The methods and techniques developed and fully detailed in this book have been instrumental in reducing (and then successfully eliminating or "banishing") his previous constant worry and anxiety.

Of course, your situation and life circumstances will depend upon a number of different and very unique (to you) factors, and therefore your results and outcomes may well vary from that of the author's and can never in any way be guaranteed.

However, it is the author's hope that this book will help the reader to take a big step forward in their unique journey to reduce or eliminate their worry and anxiety, without the need of a psychology degree, or to understand the many complex psychological terms and concepts that have been researched in order to produce this book.

To be clear, this book, and its content, is provided for educational and self-development purposes only; it is not intended to provide any medical or professional advice or guidance of any kind and is not intended for the treatment or cure of any illness, disease, or medical or psychological condition.

You should always do your own suitable and sufficient due diligence and risk assessment, and consult with your physician or professional healthcare advisor, prior to using any of the methods or techniques or products detailed or referenced in this book, and ensure that they are appropriate, suitable, and applicable for your own needs and purposes, situation, and circumstances.

Like most technologies, nothing is for everyone, and it is essential that you take note of any safety or health warning notices that are provided with any subliminal audio or visual programs (or products), and note that suffers of epilepsy are generally advised (by the product providers) not to use them.

139

It is also worth noting that during the extensive research it was found that not all brainwave entrainment, or subliminal audio or visual programs (or products), are the same; they can vary considerably in terms of quality, and therefore potential risks, as well as the technology used.

With the carefully selected UK-sourced products that the author continues to use every day, you can clearly see and review the subliminal messages you are using, which is so important since you should always be certain of what exactly you are exposing your subconscious mind to.

We suggest therefore, that you should only use products that you know are from a reliable, recognized, established, and reputable sound engineering laboratory or studio.

Affiliate disclaimer

Some of the links in this book or related references are *affiliate links*, links with a special tracking code that means, if you follow them and purchase the item using the link, we may, or may not, receive an affiliate commission.

The price of the item is exactly the same to you whether it is purchased through our affiliate link or not. We only ever suggest or recommend a product or service if we use them ourselves, or if we believe they will be of assistance and value to you and the readers of this book.

By using the *affiliate links*, you are helping, in a small way, to support the cost of the administration and research and production of this book, and the related website material, hosting and administration costs etc. We genuinely appreciate and thank you for your support.

References

1. Harvard Medical School, Harvard Health Publishing, "Anxiety and Physical Illness." July 2008 (https://www.health.harvard.edu/staying-healthy/anxiety_and_physical_illness).
    Ibid, "Understanding the Stress Response." March 2018 (https://www.health.harvard.edu/mind-and-mood/staying-healthy/understanding-the-stress-response)

2. Luana Marques PhD, "Do I Have Anxiety or Worry: What's the difference?" Harvard Medical School, Harvard Health Publishing (https://www.health.harvard.edu/blog/do-i-have-anxiety-or-worry-whats-the-difference-2018072314303)

3. WebMD, "How Worrying Affects the Body" (https://www.webmd.com/balance/guide/how-worrying-affects-your-body#1)

4. Mayo Clinic, "Anxiety Disorders, Symptoms and Causes" (https://www.mayoclinic.org/diseases-conditions/anxiety/symptoms-causes/syc-20350961)

5. James A. Blumenthal, Patrick J Smith, "Risk Factors: Anxiety and Risk of Cardiac Events." Nat Rev Cardiol. Nov 2010, 7(11):606–608

6. Benjamin B. Lahey, "Public Health Significance of Neuroticism." Am Psychol. May–Jun 2009, 64(4): 241–256

7. Pekka Jylhä, Erkki Isometsä, "The Relationship of Neuroticism and Extraversion to Symptoms of Anxiety and Depression in the General Population." Depression and Anxiety, 2006, 23:281–289

8. Sang Pyo Lee, In-Kyung Sung, Jeong Hwan Kim, Sun-Young Lee, Hyung Seok Park, Chan Sup Shim, "The Effect of Emotional Stress and Depression on the Prevalence of Digestive Diseases." J Neurogastroenterol Motil. Apr 2015, 21(2): 273–282

9. Matthew D Jacofsky Psy.D, Melanie T Santos Psy.D, Sony Khemlani-Patel PhD, Fugen Neziroglu PhD, "The Symptoms of Anxiety." Gracepoint Wellness Org, Tampa Bay's leading provider of behavioral health solutions (https://www.gracepointwellness.org/1-anxiety-disorders/article/38467-the-symptoms-of-anxiety)

10. Jacob Piet, Esben Hougaard, "The Effect of Mindfulness-Based Cognitive Therapy for Prevention of Relapse in Recurrent Major Depressive Disorder: A systematic review and meta-analysis." Clin Psychol Rev. Aug 2011, 31(6):1032–1040

11. S Helen Ma, John D Teasdale, "Mindfulness-Based Cognitive Therapy for Depression: Replication and exploration of differential relapse prevention effects." J Consult Clin Psychol. Feb 2004, 72(1):31–40

12. Stefan G Hofmann PhD, Alice T Sawyer, Ashley A Witt, Diana Oh, "The Effect of Mindfulness-Based Therapy on Anxiety and Depression: A Meta-Analytic Review." J Consult Clin Psychol. Apr 2010, 78(2):169–183

13. Richard J Davidson PhD, Jon Kabat-Zinn PhD, Jessica Schumacher MS, Melissa Rosenkranz BA, Daniel Muller MD, PhD, Saki F Santorelli EdD, Ferris Urbanowski MA, Anne Harrington PhD, Katherine Bonus MA, John F Sheridan PhD, "Alterations in Brain and Immune Function Produced by Mindfulness Meditation." Psychosom Med. Jul–Aug 2003, 65(4):564–570

14. Ljudmila Stojanovich, Dragomir Marisavljevich, "Stress as a Trigger of Autoimmune Disease." Autoimmun Rev. Feb 2008, 7(3):209–213

15. Professor Mark Williams, Dr. Danny Penman, Vidyamala Burch, "Mindfulness: Finding Peace in a Frantic World: What it can do for you." (http://franticworld.com/what-can-mindfulness-do-for-you/)

16. Jon Kabat-Zinn, *Full Catastrophe Living (Revised Edition): Using the wisdom of your body and mind to face stress, pain, and illness.* Random House Publishing Group, 2013, ISBN 9780345536938. Ibid, *Mindfulness for beginners: reclaiming the present moment – and your life.* Sounds True Inc, Har/Com Edition, 2012, ISBN: 9781604076585

17. Eckhart Tolle, *The Power of Now: A Guide to Spiritual Enlightenment.* New World Library, 2004, ISBN: 1-57731-480-8.

18. Brian G Dias, Kerry J Ressler, "Parental Olfactory Experience Influences Behavior and Neural Structure in Subsequent Generations." Nat Neurosci. Jan 2014, 17(1):89–96

19. Helen Thomson, "Study of Holocaust Survivors Finds Trauma Passed On to Children's Genes." The Guardian, 21 Aug 2015 (https://www.theguardian.com/science/2015/aug/21/study-of-holocaust-survivors-finds-trauma-passed-on-to-childrens-genes)

20. NICE Clinical Guideline "Depression in Adults: Recognition and management" (CG90). Oct 2009. Based upon evidence including Ref:11 above: S Helen Ma, John D Teasdale, "Mindfulness-Based Cognitive Therapy for Depression: Replication and exploration of differential relapse prevention effects."

21. Zindel V Segal, J Mark G Williams, John D Teasdale, *Mindfulness-Based Cognitive Therapy for Depression: A new approach to preventing relapse.* Guilford Press, 2002

22. MA Kenny, JMG Williams, "Treatment-Resistant Depressed Patients Show a Good Response to Mindfulness-Based Cognitive Therapy." Behav Res Ther, Mar 2007, 45(3):617–625

23. Willem Kuyken PhD, Fiona C Warren PhD, Rod S Taylor PhD, "Efficacy of Mindfulness-Based Cognitive Therapy in Prevention of Depressive Relapse: An individual patient data meta-analysis from randomized trials." JAMA Psychiatry, 18 Jun 2019, 73(6):565–574

24. Tara Kingston, Barbara Dooley, Anthony Bates, Elizabeth Lawlor, Kevin M Malone, "Mindfulness-Based Cognitive Therapy for Residual Depressive Symptoms." Psychology and Psychotherapy, Jul 2007, 80(2):193–203

25. Andy Shaw, *Creating A Bug Free Mind: The secret to progress.* Publisher: www.AndyShaw.com; 2nd edition, 2012, ISBN-13: 978-0957082526

26. Ruth A Baer, Gregory T Smith, Jaclyn Hopkins, Jennifer Kreitemeyer, Leslie Toney. "Using Self-Report Assessment Methods to Explore Facets of Mindfulness." Assessment, Mar 2006, 13(1):27–45

27. Amishi P Jha, Jason Krompinger, Michael J Baime, "Mindfulness Training Modifies Subsystems of Attention." Cognitive, Affective and Behavioral Neuroscience, 2007, 7:109–119

28. Yi-Yuan Tang, Yinghua Ma, Junhong Wang, Yaxin Fan, Shigang Feng, Qilin Lu, Qingbao Yu, Danni Sui, Mary K Rothbart, Ming Fan, Michael I Posner, "Short-Term Meditation Training Improves Attention and Self-Regulation." Proc Natl Acad Sci USA, Oct 23 2007, 104(43):17152–17156

29. Sadhguru Jaggi Vasudev, "Organize Your Mind And You Will Getting Anything You Want In Life," May 2018, [2,721,354 views] (https://www.youtube.com/watch?v=IKlvTQSwub8)

30. JA Brefczynski-Lewis, A Lutz, HS Schaefer, DB Levinson, RJ Davidson, "Neural Correlates of Attentional Expertise in Long-Term Meditation Practitioners." Proc Natl Acad Sci USA, 2007, 104(27):11483–11488

31. B Ivanowski, GS Malhi, "The Psychological and Neuro-Physiological Concomitants of Mindfulness Forms of Meditation." Acta Neuropsychiatrica, 2007, 19:76–91

32. Britta K Hölzel, Ulrich Ott, Tim Gard, Hannes Hempel, Martin Weygandt, Katrin Morgen, Dieter Vaitl, "Investigation of Mindfulness Meditation Practitioners with Voxel-Based Morphometry." Soc Cogn Affect Neuroscience, Mar 2008, 3(1):55–61

33. Sara W Lazar, Catherine E Kerr, Rachel H Wasserman, Jeremy R Gray, Douglas N Greve, Michael T Treadway, Metta McGarvey, Brian T Quinn, Jeffery A Dusek, Herbert Benson, Scott L Rauch, Christopher I Moore, Bruce Fischl B, "Meditation Experience is Associated with Increased Cortical Thickness." NeuroReport, Nov 28 2005, 16(17):1893–1897

34. Eileen Luders, Arthur W Toga, Natasha Lepore, Christian Gaser, "The Underlying Anatomical Correlates of Long-Term Meditation: Larger hippocampal and frontal volumes of gray matter." Neuroimage, Apr 15 2009, 45(3):672–678.

35. The Norwegian University of Science and Technology (NTNU), "Brain Waves and Meditation." ScienceDaily, Mar 31 2010 (https://www.sciencedaily.com/releases/2010/03/100319210631.htm)

36. Jenny Gu, Clara Strauss, Rod Bond, Kate Cavanagh, "How Do Mindfulness-Based Cognitive Therapy and Mindfulness-Based Stress Reduction Improve Mental Health and Wellbeing? A systematic review and meta-analysis of mediation studies." Clin Psychol Rev. Apr 2015, 37:1–12

37. Vijaya Manicavasgar, Gordon Parker, Tania Perich, "Mindfulness-Based Cognitive Therapy vs Cognitive Behaviour Therapy as a Treatment for Non-Melancholic Depression." J Affect Disord. Apr 2011, 130(1–2):138–144

38. Dawn Querstret, Mark Cropley, "Assessing Treatments Used to Reduce Rumination and/or Worry: A systematic review." Clin Psychol Rev. Aug 2013, 33(8):996–1009

39. Edson C. Tandoc Jr, Patrick Ferrucci, Margaret Duffy, "Facebook Use, Envy, and Depression Among College Students: Is Facebooking depressing?" Computers in Human Behavior, Feb 2015, 43:139–146

40. Wake Forest University Baptist Medical Center, "Anxious? Activate Your Anterior Cingulate Cortex With a Little Meditation." Jun 4 2013 (https://medicalxpress.com/news/2013-06-anxious-anterior-cingulate-cortex-meditation.html)

41. Tara Swart, "The 4 Underlying Principles of Changing Your Brain." Forbes, Mar 2018 (https://www.forbes.com/sites/taraswart/2018/03/27/the-4-underlying-principles-to-changing-your-brain/#545b243d5a71)

42. H Stokes PhD, K Ward PhD, "Neural Plasticity: 4 Steps to Change Your Brain & Habits." Authenticity Associates, June 2010 (https://www.authenticityassociates.com/neural-plasticity-4-steps-to-change-your-brain/)

43. Joseph Murphy PhD DD, *The Power of Your Subconscious Mind.* Jeremy P Tarcher, 2009, ISBN 9781585427680

44. Inspire3 Ltd, 20–22 Wenlock Street, London, N1 7GU, United Kingdom, "The Brain Evolution System" (https://www.brainev.com)

45. Fadel Zeidan, Katherine T Martucci, Robert A Kraft, John G McHaffie, Robert C Coghill, "Neural Correlates of Mindfulness Meditation-Related Anxiety Relief." Soc Cogn Affect Neurosci. Jun 2014, 9(6):751–759

46. Norman F Dixon, *Preconscious Processing.* John Wiley & Sons, 1982, ISBN 978-0471279822

47. Eldon Taylor, "Subliminal Information Theory Revisited: Casting Light on a Controversy." *Annals of the American Psychotherapy Association*, 2007, 10(3):29–33

48. Brook A Marcks, Douglas W Woods, "A Comparison of Thought Suppression to an Acceptance-Based Technique in the Management of Personal Intrusive Thoughts: A controlled evaluation." Behav Res Ther., Apr 2005, 43(4):433–45

49. Robert A Emmons, Michael E McCullough, "Counting Blessings Versus Burdens: An experimental investigation of gratitude and subjective well-being in daily life." Journal of Personality and Social Psychology, 2003, 84(2):377–389

50. Lauren Jessen, "The Benefits of a Gratitude Journal and How to Maintain One." HuffPost, 2016 Jul 8 (https://www.huffpost.com/entry/gratitude-journal_b_7745854)

51. Courtney E Ackerman, MSc, "Gratitude Journal: A collection of 67 templates, ideas, and apps for your diary." Jan 30 2021 (https://positivepsychology.com/gratitude-journal)

52. Inspire3 Ltd, 20–22 Wenlock Road, London, "Subliminal Guru." Stop worrying, alleviate your anxieties with subliminal messages. (https://SubliminalGuru.com)

53. Inspire3 Ltd, 20–22 Wenlock Road, London, "Zen12." A simple program that meditates for you and takes the hassle out of meditation. Each 12-minute session brings the benefit of an hour's advanced meditation. (https://zen12.com)

54. Inspire3 Ltd, 20–22 Wenlock Road, London. "Subliminal360." Uncover the software that changes your life while you use your computer. (https://subliminal360.com)

55. Alan J Gelenberg MD, "Psychiatric and Somatic Markers of Anxiety: Identification and pharmacologic treatment." Prim Care Companion J Clin Psychiatry, Apr 2000, 2(2):49–54

56. Edmund Jacobson, *Progressive Relaxation*. University of Chicago Press, 2nd Revised edition, 1938. ISBN: 0226390586

57. Arlin Cuncic (medically reviewed by Steven Gans MD), "How to Practice Progressive Muscle Relaxation: A step-by-step plan to relax your body." Verywell mind, Aug 2020 (https://www.verywellmind.com/how-do-i-practice-progressive-muscle-relaxation-3024400)

A Final Word

If you have any questions regarding the content, or suggestions to make of this book, you can contact me at support@thebestyouprogramme.com and I will attempt to assist you in any way I can. Please allow up to seven calendar days for a response.

I sincerely wish you well in your journey to free yourself from your worry and anxiety, and I applaud you for having the courage and determination to keep yourself moving toward achieving the sheer bliss that only a worry and anxiety free state of mind can give you.

Even if this book has only helped you to take a few steps along that journey, then my endeavors over the past two-plus years have all been worthwhile.

If you enjoyed this book, or found it helpful, it would mean the world to me if you would leave a short review, and please do share it with anyone you think might benefit from it.

Remember: to get the very best from the LENSE+GP method, and to do so with the least amount of effort, it is essential that you download and use your FREE Zen12 meditation with brainwave entrainment MP3 audio.

The highly specialized Zen12 audio should, at the very least, save you the considerable time and effort it would otherwise take you to learn (and become proficient in) meditation, at the level needed to achieve the deeply relaxed state of mind that is required for you to successfully and consistently apply the thought control technique of "No-Mind," as described in this book.

Like many things in life, the more you use it, the easier it becomes, and the better your results.

Your FREE Zen12 download audio has been specially arranged with the UK specialized producer and provider of this highly respected software, for readers of this book, via our website.

To access your own FREE downloadable copy of the brainwave enhanced Zen12 guided meditation track, simply download it by going direct to the website at:

https://www.zen12.com/gift/a/thebestyou

or alternatively visit our website:

https://www.thebestyouprogramme.com/book/free-mp3

where you can register for free updates, other helpful resources, and FREE information… so register, download, and enjoy!

Other helpful resources

If you are interested in the more advanced, and more expensive, Brain Evolution System,[44] you can get all of the details by visiting the following site:

https://www.brainev.com/gift/a/thebestyou

or alternatively visit our website at:

https://www.thebestyouprogramme.com/book/brain-evolution-system

Finally… should you be interested in losing weight, or in internet · marketing, please do take a look at our sister websites for the "Best" and latest research and information available at:

www.thebestweightlossprogramme.com

or:

www.thebestinternetmarketingprogramme.com

Finally… finally… from everyone associated with the "Best Programs," we truly wish you the very best. Please always stay safe and continue to strive to be the very best that you can be, and to live your life fully as it was intended to be.

Index

Printed in Great Britain
by Amazon